An Arran Anthology

Hamish Whyte

Born 1947. Lives and works in Glasgow. Married with two children. Holidays in Arran every year. Edited *The Scottish Cat* (1987), *Mungo's Tongues: Glasgow Poems 1630-1990* (1993) and many other anthologies. Compiled Scots and Gaelic versions of *The Minister's Cat* (1991 and 1994), illustrated by Barbara Robertson. With Catherine Brown co-edited *A Scottish Feast: An Anthology of Food and Eating* (1996). Writes occasional poems. Currently translating Martial.

In memory of my father
James Halley Whyte
and happy days on Arran

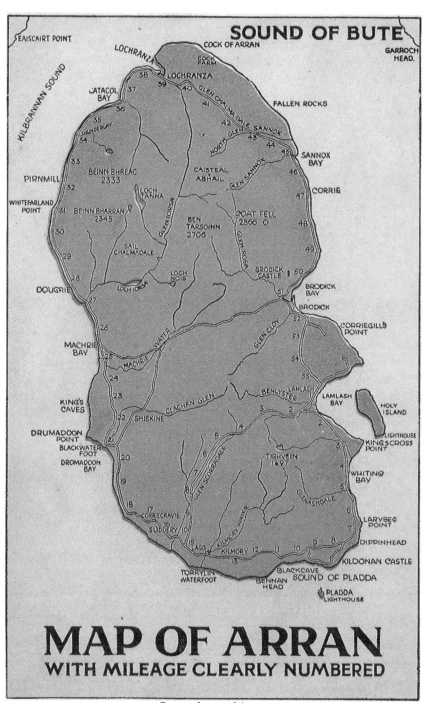

Postcard map of Arran

An Arran
Anthology

edited by
Hamish Whyte

MERCAT PRESS
EDINBURGH

First published in 1997 by Mercat Press
James Thin, 53 South Bridge, Edinburgh EH1 1YS

ISBN 1873644 671

The editor and publisher gratefully acknowledge the
following for allowing copyright material to be re-
printed: Little, Brown (for Iain Banks), HarperCollins
(for George Blake), George Bruce, Thomas A. Clark,
Robin Fulton, Nora Hunter (for Margaret Hamilton),
Carl MacDougall, James McGonigal, John McLellan (for
Robert McLellan), Naomi Mitchison, Edwin Morgan,
Lesley Bratton (for Neil Munro), Alison Prince,
Canongate Books (for Alastair Reid), Archie E. Roy,
Pat Sillars (for John Sillars).
We apologise to anyone omitted from the above and
would be pleased to be notified of any corrections.

The drawings on pp. 6, 15, 19, 28, 57, 121 are taken from
George Milner, *Studies of Nature on the Coast of Arran*, 1894

Set in Palatino at Mercat Press
Printed and bound in Great Britain by
Athenæum Press Ltd., Gateshead, Tyne & Wear

Contents

List of Illustrations   xi
Acknowledgements   xii
Introduction   xiii
Editor's Note   *xv*

ANONYMOUS
Arran of the Many Stags (12th century)   1
JOHN BARBOUR
The Bruce on Arran (1374-75)   1
DONALD MONRO
Ane Grate Ile (1549)   4
GEORGE BUCHANAN
Abundant Fishing (1582)   6
WILLIAM LITHGOW
This Isle of Arran (1628)   6
MARTIN MARTIN
A Description of Arran (1695)   7
GLASGOW JOURNAL
Goat Milk Quarters (1759)   11
THOMAS PENNANT
A Scene of Savage Sterility (1772)   11
[MR HUTCHISON]
A February Jaunt (1783)   16
REV. JAMES HEADRICK
View of the Island of Arran (1803)   18
SIR WALTER SCOTT
Bruce Steers for Arran's Isle (1815)   23
JOHN PHILLIPS
Various Instructive Phenomena (1826)   24
REV. DAVID LANDSBOROUGH
Thou Majestic Arran (1828)   25

John Wilson
Was There a Bonnier Sight (1829)   29
William Wordsworth
On the Frith of Clyde (1833)   29
John Paterson
The People of Arran (1834)   30
Elizabeth King
Summers by the Sea (1834)   31
Lord Teignmouth
Sketches of Arran (1836)   34
Elvira Anna Phipps
The Ascent of Goatfell (1840)   36
Andrew Ramsay
Corrie An Lochan (1841)   37
Henry, Lord Cockburn
A Taste for the Tops of Hills (1842)   38
Ayr Observer
Brodick Fair (1847)   42
J. Smith
A Week in Arran (1847)   43
Anonymous
A Tamer Scene (1848)   48
Alexander Smith
Glen Sannox (1848)   50
John Fergusson
On Seeing the Tower of Pladda Lit for the First Time (1849)   52
Thomas Alexander
Picnic at King's Cove (1853)   54
Anonymous
Sweet Arran's Isle (1859)   55
Lewis Carroll
A Delightful Visit to Lamlash (1871)   56
William Mitchell
Glen Sannox Adventure (1874)   57
William Thomson
Goatfell (1876)   63
William Lytteil
The Picture Cave (1877)   63
John T. Reid
Art Rambles (1878)   65
William McQueen
To Parties in Search of a Cheap Holiday (c.1880)   67
William Brown Smith
A Ramble Round Arran (1882)   70

C.T. BORRIE
Lamlash Churchyard (1882) 76
ALEXANDER MAC LACHLAN
The Kye Song (1888) 76
ALEXANDER G. MURDOCH
Lodgings at Arran (1888) 78
THE SCOTSMAN AND GLASGOW HERALD
The Arran Murder (1889) 82
CHARLES E. HALL
The Kirn Supper (1893) 88
GEORGE MILNER
Characters (1894) 91
GEORGE EYRE-TODD
Sheep-Shearing in Arran (1895) 94
ALEXANDER CARMICHAEL
Fairy Stories (1895) 97
STAZEL DENE
Hamish at the Glen (1898) 100
'HARI- KARI' (ROBERT BROWNING)
The Heliotrope Bretelles (1910) 101
T.C.F. BROTCHIE
A Strange Story (1911) 101
WILLIAM BROWN
Wild Monamore (1912) 102
PADDY COFFEY
The Arran Smacks (c.1920) 103
NEIL MUNRO
Isle of Arran (1923) 104
'R. M. FEATHERPICK'
The Bonny Lads o' Corrie (1923) 107
JOHN SILLARS
Common Things Like Stick Gathering (1925) 109
JAMES NICOL
To an Arran Piermaster (1930) 114
JOHN JOY BELL
Isle of Arran (1933) 115
NAOMI MITCHISON
From The Alban Goes Out (1939) 116
ALASDAIR ALPIN MACGREGOR
Lochranza Brambles, etc. (1948) 118
MARGARET HAMILTON
Servant of the Lord (1950) 122
GEORGE BLAKE
Arran Villages (1952) 125

Robert McLellan
Arran Burn: A Poem for Television (1965)   130
Archie Roy
Victim Running (1968)   135
George Bruce
Coach Tour and Locals (1969)   140
Alistair Reid
Isle of Arran (1978)   140
Robin Fulton
Flying Over Arran (1979)   141
Arran Haiku (c.1980)   142
Hamish Whyte
Siva in Lamlash (1982)   143
Edwin Morgan
Arran Potatoes (1985)   144
Iain Banks
The Sleeping Warrior (1986)   144
Thomas A. Clark
Coire Fhionn Lochan (1990)   145
Alison Prince
Holy Isle (1991)   146
Carl MacDougall
Thinking of Coire Fhionn Lochan (1996)   147
James McGonigal
The Old Song (1997)   147

Postscript   149
Glossary   150
Notes   152
Bibliography and Further Reading   155
Index   163

Illustrations

Brodick Castle   3
Blaeu's Map of Arran   5
Arran from the Sea   6
Lochranza Bay, with Basking Sharks   12
Lamlash   15
Sea Fishing   19
The Saddle and Cir-Mhor   28
Corrie an Lachan   38
View From Summit of Goat Fell   41
Fishermen's Huts   45
Holy Island   57
The Boat-house   65
Goatfell and Brodick Sands   79
The Lagg Hotel   88
Flock of Sheep in Glen Rosa   95
Castle and Lochranza Bay   103
Fullarton's Cart   105
Steamer in Brodick Bay   114
North Sannox Shore   121
The Agricultural Show   124
Whiting Bay   127
Bungalow Road, Lamlash   143
Standing Stones, Machrie Moor   148
The Beach, Lamlash   149

Acknowledgements

First of all, a thank you to the many people and places that have made visiting Arran a pleasure over the years, especially: Janet Cowley, Irene and Sandy Sillars, Mr and Mrs Matt Kerr, Cathy Mackenzie, Mr and Mrs Dick (of Clifton Hotel), Lynn Ross, Bill Gunn, the Alexander Brothers (not the singing ones), Stephen Gill, Owen Swindale, John and Patricia Young, the Coffee Pot, the Anvil Tea Room, Studio 4, the Nature Centre, and not forgetting the Whyte and Walker families.

Thanks for supplying me with Arran books to Cooper Hay, Adam McNaughtan, Audrey McCrone, Book and Card Centre, Brodick.

I am also grateful to the Mitchell Library, Glasgow, for allowing its resources to be plundered for text and illustrations and to the Document Delivery Service of Glasgow University Library for tracking down out-of-the-way items.

Special thanks to Colin Cowley for his assistance and for his very useful *Arran Books File*, and to John Kilkie and Hazel Wright for reading the text and offering helpful comment.

Thanks also to the following for help and encouragement: Simon Berry, Moira Burgess, Karen Cunningham, Donny O'Rourke, Edwin Morgan, Alan and Helen Durndell, Anne Escott, David McMenemy, Cordelia Oliver, Robert Walker, David Hamilton and George Fairfull-Smith (for his list of Arran paintings).

To Seán Costello and Tom Johnstone of Mercat Press for their always amiable attention and care, many thanks.

And, as ever, to Winifred, the gratefulness is terrific!

Introduction

Seperately and together my wife and I have been going to Arran for our holidays for nearly fifty years, and both of our families before us. As with most visitors to the island, no matter how constant, we can never become 'local', we remain incomers. Even if we lived there, we would always be outsiders. This is not meant as criticism, it's just how things are. Perhaps it's part of the attraction. Perhaps if we lived there the island might lose its magic.

Certainly Arran has always figured more as a place to visit than to live. The earliest proper reference to the island—in the St Patrick literature—describes it as a hunting ground for the Irish. Robert the Bruce found it a convenient stopping place in his campaign of 1307. From the seventeenth century it became a resort for the curious traveller, the tourist and eventually the modern holiday-maker (of whom there are now 240,000 a year according to a report in the *Arran Banner* of 1 February 1997).

For whatever reasons, the island has long exerted a fascination (I don't propose to try to analyse this) and must be one of the most written-about islands in the world (Skye would be another). Surely no holiday resort can boast a greater literature? Very little of that literature has been written by native Arranites (only the novelist John Sillars and the poet Robin Fulton come to mind). But an endless stream of visitors came—to better their health, to marvel at the mountains, to 'improve' conditions, to collect seaweed, to watch birds, to get away from it all, to ramble, to idle, to paint, to write, to retire—the agenda as various as the visitors—and felt compelled to write about their visit. From Caeilte's 'delectable isle' Arran has inspired cliché after cliché: 'Scotland in miniature', 'Scotland's Holiday Isle', 'An Island to Treasure'—it has something for everyone, and yet, at least in today's variety-packed holiday market, it has very little—just an indefinable attraction.

I do not claim to be an expert on Arran, only someone who loves the island and who has collected books and other material about it for many years. Real experts are listed in the bibliography—many experts are not listed anywhere. However, most of the modern books about Arran are able only to quote briefly from or merely mention the previous literature, much of which is not easily accessible. This anthology offers a chance to read people like Martin, Pennant, Headrick, Landsborough, Sillars and others at greater length, to get more of their flavour, to follow first hand the accounts of early tourists, to form a better impression of the poetry and fiction written about the island. It is a collection of pieces about Arran, arranged roughly chronologically from medieval times to the present. It is not a history of the island, although the main elements are touched on (geology, prehistory, the Bruce, the Dukes of Hamilton, the 'improvements', the Clearances, the growth of tourism)—for the best all round picture of Arran the reader should go to Robert McLellan's marvellous *The Isle of Arran*. This book is more of a ragbag of stories, poems, impressions, memoirs and adventures. I hope it illustrates the diversity of writing about Arran—as well as the similarities: there seems to be a recurring compulsion, for example, to write about climbing Goatfell—the ascent of, the view from, this Corbett (not even a Munro) has provoked torrents of sublime gush—ample testimony, I suppose, to the fact that it *is* sublime!

The original idea was to include mainly poetry and fiction, but there are so many interesting documentary accounts of the island by visitors that I felt they should have a place also. Many of these visitors were famous in their own right: Wordsworth (who compared Arran to Tenerife!), Lord Cockburn, Thomas Carlyle, Lewis Carroll, Robert Browning. In a letter of 1876 to Annie Egerton Smith, with whom he and his sister had stayed on Arran, Browning wrote: 'Two days ago I called on dear old Carlyle, & walked out with him. I wanted to hear what he remembered of Arran whence (you remember) he had written me such pleasant letters long years ago. To my sorrow—& almost consternation—he had forgotten he was ever there: said, with a smile, "It is a lapsed memory."' It is pleasant to think of two of the giants of Victorian literature discussing Arran in London. Confirmation that Browning was indeed on Arran comes from *Arran in Spring* (1937) edited by Charles Ker, a record of visits to Arran from 1879 to 1937. He records that his brother W.P. Ker (to be famous himself as a scholar) in 1876 aged about twenty-one, 'walking on the Lamlash road with his cousin Emma Johnston and Ada Maxwell, met Robert Browning. W.P. having been well brought up, raised his hat to the distinguished poet, and after he had passed turned and made a deep bow to his back, saying, "That is the greatest man in the world."'

Keats never visited Arran, but noticed the island when he was in Ayrshire paying his respects at Burns's birthplace: 'there were the Mountains of Arran Isle, black and huge over the sea' (letter to John Reynolds, 11 July 1818). Much has been made of the fact that Burns himself never mentioned Arran despite its obvious presence in his landscape. But why should he? Burns did, in fact, have a couple of Arran connections. While he was in

Irvine learning the flax dressing he met Willie Davidson, wheelwright, of Glen Rosa. And 'Highland Mary' (Margaret Campbell) was in service at one time to the Rev. David Campbell of Lochranza, a relative of her mother. Artists, too, found Arran congenial: Horatio McCulloch, Noel Paton, John T. Reid, Joan Eardley, Craigie Aitchison, Mairi Hedderwick and many others, both amateur and professional.

These visitors and the accounts of travellers like Martin Martin and Thomas Pennant encouraged others to visit the island. There were also the dreaded 'improvers' such as John Burrel, the Rev. James Headrick and the factor John Paterson, who changed the farming system, cleared the people and tried to stamp out the Gaelic language (though Headrick, in Utopian mood, wanted everyone to speak the same language—English, of course— so that they would 'be one people'). And geologists, like James Hutton and Andrew Ramsay; and naturalists such as the famous Landsboroughs, father and son—their writings may be clogged with piety and lists of algae, but they were alive to Arran's beauty and fairly convey their enthusiasm.

Artists and authors are still attracted to Arran. Robert McLellan lived a good part of his life at High Corrie. Alison Prince lives in Whiting Bay. The artist Lesley Mann has recently moved to Brodick. The island seems to be a potter's paradise, from Hugh Purdie and Alasdair Dunn to Lindsay Hamilton and Carol Furze. It's chock-a-block with crafts, from weaving to stained glass.

Arran, of course, is not only for artists and authors—they just make their impressions public. There are also hundreds of thousands of other Arrans— in snapshots, postcards and people's memories—each person has his or her own Arran anthology. I hope you like this one.

Hamish Whyte
February 1997

Editor's Note

I have interfered with the original texts as little as possible, occasionally changing punctuation and correcting printers' errors and rationalising capitalisation in the earlier extracts, for the sake of clarity. * generally indicates a long break between passages, ... a shorter. Spellings of place names, which can vary from author to author, have not been 'corrected', but they are given in the index in their currently accepted form. This is not a scholarly edition: the notes and glossary are pretty basic. I hope the reader will be encouraged to explore further, using the bibliography.

Arran of the Many Stags

Anonymous, 12th century

Patrick said again: 'it is well, Caeilte; what was the best hunting that the Fianna ever had, whether in Ireland or in Scotland?' 'The hunting of Arran.' Patrick enquired: 'where is that land?' 'Betwixt Scotland and Pictland: on the first day of the *trogan*-month (which now is called *lughnasadh* i.e. "Lammas-tide") we, to the number of the Fianna's three battalions, practised to repair thither and there have our fill of hunting until such time as from the tree-tops the cuckoo would call in Ireland. More melodious than all music whatsoever it was to give ear to the voices of the birds as they rose from the billows and from the island's coast-line; thrice fifty separate flocks there were that encircled her, and they clad in gay brilliance of all colours: as blue, and green, and azure, and yellow.' Here Caeilte uttered a lay: 'Arran of the many stags—the sea impinges on her very shoulders! An island in which whole companies were fed—and with ridges among which blue spears are reddened! Skittish deer are on her pinnacles, soft blackberries on her waving heather; cool water there is in her rivers, and mast upon her russet oaks! Greyhounds there were in her, and beagles; blaeberries and sloes of the dark blackthorn; dwellings with their backs set close against her woods, and the deer fed scattered by her oaken thickets! A crimson crop grew on her rocks, in all her glades a faultless grass; over her crags affording friendly refuge, leaping went on and fawns were skipping! Smooth were her level spots—her wild swine, they were fat; cheerful her fields (this is a tale that may be credited), her nuts hung on her forest-hazels' boughs, and there was sailing of long galleys past her! Right pleasant their condition all when the fair weather sets in: under her rivers' brinks trouts lie; the seagulls wheeling round her grand cliff answer one the other—at every fitting time delectable is Arran!'

From *The Colloquy* [Anon. 12th century] in *Silva Gadelica: a collection of tales in Irish* edited from MSS and translated by Standish H. O'Grady (Williams and Norgate, 1892)

The Bruce on Arran

John Barbour (1374-75)

To King Robert again we go, who lay in Rathlin with his company till the winter was near gone, and took his provision from that island.

James of Douglas was vexed that they should lie idle so long, and he said to Sir Robert Boyd, 'The poor folk of this country are at great charge for us, who lie idle here. And I hear say that in Arran, in a strong castle of stone, are Englishmen who by force hold the lordship of the island. Go we thither, and it may well befall that we shall trouble them in some way.'

Sir Robert said, 'To that I agree. There were little reason in lying longer here. Therefore will we pass to Arran, for I know that country right well, and the castle also. We shall come there so privily, that they shall have no sight or news of our coming. And we shall lie ambushed near, where we may see their coming out. So it shall nowise fail but we shall do them damage of some sort.' With that they made ready anon, and took their leave of the king, and went forth on their way.

They came soon to Cantyre, then rowed always by the land till near night, when they made their way to Arran. There they arrived safely, and drew their galley under a hillside, and there covered it up. Their tackle, oars, and rudder they hid in the same fashion, and held their way in the dead of night, so that, ere daylight dawned, they were in skilful ambush near the castle. There, though they were wet and weary, and hungry with long fasting, they planned to hold themselves all privy till they could see their proper chance.

Sir John the Hastings was at that that time in the castle of Brodick, with knights of high pride, and squires, and good yeomanry, a very great company. And often at his pleasure he went hunting with his followers, and held the land in such subjection that none durst refuse to do his will. He was still in the castle when James of Douglas laid his ambush, as I have said.

By chance it so happened at that time that close to the place of the ambush the under-warden had arrived the evening before with three boats loaded with victual and provision, clothing and arms. Douglas soon saw thirty and more Englishmen go from the boats loaded with sundry stuff. Some carried wine and some arms. A number were loaded with stores of different sort, and various others marched idly by them, like masters.

The men in ambush saw them, and without fear or awe, broke from hiding, and slew all they could overtake. Then rose an outcry loud and terrible, for the men of the boats, in fear of death, roared aloud like beasts. Douglas's followers slew without pause or mercy, so that very nigh forty English lay dead.

When those in the castle heard the outcry and uproar they sallied forth to the fight. But Douglas, seeing them, rallied his men, and went hastily to meet them. And when the garrison saw him come fearlessly at them, they fled without more fighting, their assailants following them to the gate, and slaying them as they passed in. But those in flight barred the gate so quickly that the pusuers could not get at them further. Therefore they left them and turned again to the sea, where the men were slain before. And when the English in the boats saw them coming, and knew in what fashion they had

2

Brodick Castle, 1790 (from F. Grose, Antiquities of Scotland, *1789-91)*

discomfited their fellows, they put hastily to sea, and rowed diligently with all their might. But the wind was against them, and it raised such breakers that they could in no wise get out to sea. Neither durst they come to land, but held themselves plunging there so long that two of the three boats were swamped. When Douglas saw this, he took the arms and clothing, victual, wine, and other stores which he found at the place, and went his way, right joyful and pleased with the plunder.

Thus James of Douglas and his company, by God's grace, were fully furnished with stores of arms, clothing, and provisions. Then they held their way to a narrow place, and stoutly maintained themselves, till on the tenth day the king with all his following arrived in that region.

Bruce reached Arran with thirty-three small galleys, and landed and took up his quarters in a steading. There he enquired particularly if any had tidings of strangers in the island.

'Yes, sir,' said a woman, 'I can indeed tell you of strangers arrived in this country. A short while since, by their valour, they discomfited our warden and slew many of his men. In a strong place at hand the whole company has its resort.' 'Dame,' said the king, 'do thou make known to me the place of their retreat, and I shall reward thee indeed; for they are all of my house, and most glad would I be to set eyes on them, as, certainly I know, would they be to set eyes on me.' 'Sir,' said she, 'I will blithely go with you and your company till I show you their quarters.' 'That is enough, my fair sister,' said the king. 'Now let us go forward.' Without more delay then they marched after her, till at last she showed the king the place in a woody glen. 'Sir,' she said, 'here I saw the men ye ask after make their lodging; here I trow, is their retreat.' The king then blew his horn, and made the men beside him keep still and hidden. Then again he blew his horn.

James of Douglas heard him blow, and at once knew the blast, and said, 'Assuredly yonder is the king; many a day have I known his blowing.'

Therewith the Bruce blew a third time. Then Sir Robert Boyd knew it, and said, 'Yonder, for certain, is the king. Go we forth to him with all speed.'

They hastened to the king, and saluted him most courteously. And Bruce welcomed them gladly, and was joyful of their meeting, and kissed them, and enquired how they had fared in their hunting. And they told him everything truly, and praised God that they had met. Then, gay and glad at heart, they went with the king to his quarters.

John Barbour (c.1316-1396) *The Bruce* (1374-75). Translated by George Eyre-Todd (Glasgow, 1907)

Ane Grate Ile
Donald Monro, 1549

Be north or northeast fra [Islay], twenty-four myles of sea, lyes Arran, ane grate ile, full of grate montans and forrests, good for hunting, with pairt of woods, extending in lenthe from the Kyle of Arran to castle Dounan southwart to twenty-four myles, and from the Kyle of Drumdouin to the Ness of Kilbride sixteen myles of breadthe, inhabit onlie at the sea-coasts. Herein are thre castils: ane callit Braizay, pertening to the Earle of Arran; ane uther auld house callit the castle of the heid of Lochrenasay, pertyning likeways to the said Earle; and the third callit castle Dou[n]an, pertaining to ane of the Stuarts of Bute's blood, callit Mr James, he and his bluid are the best men in that countrey. In Arran is a loche callit Lochrenasay, with three or four small waters. Twa paroch-kirks, the ane callit Kilbride, the uther callit Kylmure …. Upone the shore of this iyle lyes Flada, ane little iyle full of cunings, with ane uther little ile callit the yle of Molass, quherin ther was foundit by Johne Lord of the isles ane monastry of friars, which is decayit.

Donald Monro, Dean of the Isles (fl.1550-1574) *Description of the Western Isles of Scotland called Hybrides* [1549] (Edinburgh: William Auld, 1774)

ARRAN.

Blaeu's Map, 1654 (from The Book of Arran, v. II, 1914)

[From 'Blaeu's Atlas,' 1654.

Abundant Fishing

George Buchanan, 1582

About twenty-five miles north from Ailsa, lies the isle of Arran, twenty-four miles long, and sixteen broad. It rises every where into high and rugged mountains. The sea coast only is inhabited. Where it is lowest the sea forms a pretty large bay, whose entrance is protected by the island Molas, besides which, the mountains towering on every side break the force of the wind, and render it a very safe harbour for shipping. In these waters, perpetually tranquil, the fishing is so abundant, that if more be caught than what are required for one day, the inhabitants throw them back again into the sea, as into a fish pond. Not far from Arran lies the little island Flada, swarming with rabbits.

George Buchanan (1506-1582) *The History of Scotland* [1582]. Translated from the Latin by James Aikman (Glasgow and Edinburgh, 1827)

This Isle of Arran

William Lithgow, 1628

I arrived, I say, at the isle of Arran, *anno* 1628, where for certain days, in the castle of Braidwick, I was kindly entertained by the illustrious Lord James, Marquis of Hamilton, Earl of Arran and Cambridge, etc.

This isle of Arran, is thirty miles long, eight in breadth, and distant from the main twenty four miles; being surclouded with Goatfield hill, which, with wide eyes, overlooketh the western continent, and the northern country of Ireland: bringing also to sight, in a clear summer day, the isle of Man, and the higher coast of Cumberland. A larger prospect no mountain in the world can show, pointing out three kingdoms at one sight; neither is there any isle like to it, for brave gentry, good archers, and hill-hovering hunters.

William Lithgow (1582-c.1645) *Travels and Voyages* (Edinburgh, 1770)

Arran from the Sea by W. Noel Johnson, 1894

A Description of Arran

Martin Martin, 1695

The name of this isle is by some derived from *Arran*, which in the Irish language signifies Bread. Others think it comes more probably from *Arin*, or *Arfyn*, which in their language is as much as the place of the giant Fin-Mac-Cowl's slaughter or execution; for *Aar* signifies Slaughter, and so they will have *Arin* only the contraction of *Arrin* or *Fin*; the received tradition of the great giant Fin-Mac-Cowl's military valour, which he exercised upon the ancient natives here, seems to favour this conjecture; this they say is evident from the many stones set up in divers places of the isle, as monuments upon the graves of persons of note that were kill'd in battle. This isle is twenty four miles from south to north, and seven miles from east to west. It lies between the Isle of Boot, and Kyntyre, in the opposite mainland. The isle is high and mountainous, but slopes on each side round the coast, and the glen is only made use of for tillage. The mountains near Brodick Bay, are of a considerable height, all the hills generally afford a good pasturage, tho' a great part of 'em be covered only with heath.

The mold here is of divers colours, being black and brown near the hills, and clayie and sandy upon the coast.

The natives told me that some places of the isle, affords fullers-earth. The coast on the east side is rockie near the shoar; the stones on the coast for some miles beneath Brodick, are all of a red colour, and of these the Castle of Brodick is built. The natives say that the mountains near the Castle of Brodick affords chrystal, and that the Dutchess of Hamilton put so great a value on it, as to be at the charge of cutting a necklace of it, which the inhabitants take as a great honour done them, because they have a great veneration for her Grace. There is no considerable woods here, but a few coppices, yet that in the glen towards the west is above a mile in length. There are capacious fields of arable ground on each side Brodick Bay, as also on the opposite western coast. The largest and best field for pasturage is that on the south-west side.

Several rivers on each side this isle affords salmon, particularly the two rivers on the west called Mackir side, and the two in Kirkmichel and Brodich Bay.

The air here is temperately cold and moist, which is in some measure qualified by the fresh breezes that blow from the hills, but the natives think a dram of strong-waters is a good corrective.

There are several caves on the coast of this isle, those on the west are pretty large, particularly that in Druim-cruey, a hundred men may sit or lie in it, it is contracted gradually from the floor upwards to the roof, in the upper-end there is a large piece of a rock form'd like a pillar, there's engraven on it a deer, and underneath it a two-handed sword; there is a void space on each side this pillar.

The southside of the cave has a horseshoe engraven on it. On each side the door, there's a hole cut out, and that they say was for holding big trees, on which the caldrons hang for boyling their beef and venison. The natives say that this was the cave in which Fin-Mac-Cowl lodged during the time of his residence in this isle, and that his guards lay in the lesser caves, which are near this big one; there is a little cave joyning to the largest, and this they call the cellar.

There is a cave some miles more southerly on the same coast, and they told me that the minister preached in it sometimes, in regard of its being more centrical than the parish church.

Several erected stones are to be seen on each side this isle; four of these are near Brodich-Bay, about the distance of 70 yards from the river, and are seven foot high each. The highest of these stones that fell under my observation was on the south-side of Kirkmichel River, and is above fifteen foot high; there is a stone coffin near it which has been fill'd with humane bones, until of late that the river washed away the earth, and the bones that were in the coffin; Mac-Loui, who had seen them, says they were of no larger size than those of our own time. On the west-side there are three stones erected in Baellimianich, and a fourth at some distance from these, about six foot high each. In the moor on the east-side Druim-cruey, there is a circle of stones, the area is about thirty paces; there is a stone of same shape and kind about forty paces to the west of the circle, the natives say that this circle was made by the giant Fin-Mac-Cowl, and that to the single stone Bran, Fin-Mac-Cowl's hunting dog was usually tied. About half a mile to the north-side Baelliminich there are two stones erected each of them eight foot high.

There is a circle of big stones a little to the south of Druim-cruey, the area of which is about twelve paces; there is a broad thin stone in the middle of this circle, supported by three lesser stones, the ancient inhabitants are reported to have burnt their sacrifices on the broad stone, in time of heathenism.

There is a thin broad stone tapering towards the top, erected within a quarter of a mile of the sea, near Machir River, and is nine foot high, and at some little distance from the river, there is a large cavern of stones.

There is an eminence of about a thousand paces in compass on the sea coast in Druim-cruey village, and it is fenced about with a stone-wall. Of old it was a sanctuary, and whatever number of men or cattle could get within, it was secured from the assaults of their enemies, the place being privileged by universal consent.

The only good harbour in this isle is Lamlash, which is in southeast end of the isle of that name.

There is a great fishing of cod and whiting, in and about this bay.

The whole isle is design'd by nature more for pasturage, than cultivation; the hills are generally covered all over with heath, and produce a mixture of the *Erica-Baccifera*, *Cats-tail* and *Juniper*, all which are very agreeable to the eye in the summer. The highest hills of this island are seen at a considerable distance from several parts of the continent and north-west isles, and they serve instead of a forrest to maintain the deer, which are about four hundred in number, and they are carefully kept by a forrester, to give sport to the Duke of Hamilton, or any of his family that go a hunting there. For if any of the natives happen to kill a deer without license, which is not often granted, he is liable to a fine of 20*l*. Scots for each deer. And when they grow too numerous, the forrester grants licenses for killing a certain number of them, on condition they bring the skins to himself.

The cattle here are horses and cows of a middle size, and they have also sheep and goats. This isle affords the common sea and land fowls that are to be had in the Western Isles. The black cock is not allow'd to be killed here without a license, the transgressors are liable to a fine.

The castle of Brodich on the north side of the bay of that name, stands on a plain, from which there is about 400 paces of a gradual descent towards the sea.

This castle is built in a long form, from south to north there is a wall of two stories high that encompasses the castle and tower; the space within the wall on the south side the castle, is capable of mustring a battalion of men.

The castle is four stories high, and has a tower of greater height joined to the north side, and that has a bastion close to it, to which a lower bastion is added. The south and west sides are surrounded with a broad wet ditch, but the east and north sides have a descent which will not admit of a wet ditch. The gate looks to the east. This castle is the Duke of Hamilton's seat, when his Grace or any of the family make their summer visit to this island. The bayliff or steward has his residence in this castle, and he has a deputation to act with full power to levy the rents, give leases of the lands, and hold courts of justice.

There is another castle belonging to the Duke in the north side the isle, at the head of Loch Kenistil, in which there is an harbour for barks and boats. The Isle of Arran is the Duke of Hamilton's property (a very small part excepted) it lies in the Sheriffdom of Boot, and made part of the Diocess of Argyle.

The inhabitants of this island are composed of several tribes. The most ancient family among them, is by the natives reckon'd to be Mack Louis, which in the ancient language signifies the son of Lewis; they own themselves to be descended of French parentage, their sirname in English is Fullerton, and their title Kirk Michell, the place of their residence. If tradition be true, this little family is said to be of 700 years standing. The present possessor oblig'd me with the sight of his old and new charters, by which he is one of the King's coroners within this island, and as such, he hath a halbert peculiar to his office; he has his right of late from the family of Hamilton, wherein his title and perquisites of coroner are confirm'd to him and his heirs. He is oblig'd to have three men to attend him upon all publick emergencies, and he is bound by his office to pursue all malefactors, and to deliver them to the steward, or in his absence to the next judge. And if any of the inhabitants refuse to pay their rents at the usual term, the coroner is bound to take him personally, or to seize his goods. And if it should happen that the coroner with his retinue of three men is not sufficient to put his office in execution, then he summons all the inhabitants to concurr with him, and immediately they rendezvous to the place, where he fixes his coroner's staff. The perquisites due to the coroner are a firlet or bushel of oats, and a lamb from every village in the isle, both which are punctually paid him at the ordinary terms.

The inhabitants of this isle are well proportion'd, generally brown, and some of a black complection; they enjoy a good state of health, and have a genius for all callings or imployments, tho' they have but few mechanicks; they wear the same habit with those of the nearest isles, and are very civil; they all speak the Irish language, yet the English tongue prevails on the east side, and ordinarily the ministers preach in it, and in Irish on the west side. Their ordinary asservation is by *Nale*, for I did not hear any oath in the island.

The churches in this isle are, Kilbride in the south east, Kilmore in the south, Cabel Uual a chapel, Kilmichel in the village of that name, St James's Church at the north end.

The natives are all Protestants, they observe the festivals of Christmas, Good-Friday, and Easter. I had like to have forgot a valuable curiosity in this isle, which they call *Baul Mulny*, i.e. Molingus his Stone Globe; this saint was chaplain to Mack Donald of the Isles; his name is celebrated here on the account of this globe, so much esteem'd by the inhabitants. This stone for its intrinsick value has been carefully transmitted to posterity for several ages. It is a green stone much like a globe in figure, about the bigness of a goose egg.

The vertues of it is to remove stiches from the sides of sick persons, by laying it close to the place affected, and if the patient does not out-live the distemper, they say the stone removes out of the bed of its own accord, and *e contra*. The natives use this stone for swearing decisive oaths upon it.

They ascribe another extraordinary vertue to it, and 'tis this; the credulous vulgar firmly believe that if this stone is cast among the front of an enemy, they will all run away, and that as often as the enemy rallies, if this stone is cast among them, they still lose courage, and retire. They say that Mackdonald of the Isles carried this stone about him, and that victory was always on his side when he threw it among the enemy. The custody of this globe is the peculiar privilege of a little family called Clan-Chattons, alias Mack Intosh, they were ancient followers of Mack Donald of the Isles. This stone is now in the custody of Margaret Millar, alias Mack Intosh, she lives in Baellmianich, and preserves the globe with abundance of care; it is wrapped up in fair linen cloath, and about that there is a piece of woollen cloath, and she keeps it still lock'd up in her chest, when it is not given out to exert its qualities.

Martin Martin (d.1719) *A Description of the Western Islands of Scotland* (London: Andrew Bell, 1703)

Goat Milk Quarters
Glasgow Journal, 1759

Good goat milk quarters may be had this season in the island of Arran, in a very commodious slated house, hard by the Castle of Brodick, consisting of three very good rooms above stairs, and two below, with a large kitchen, some bedsteads, chairs and tables. This house will serve two small families, with garden things at hand.

There is a packet boat settled to pass every week from Arran to Saltcoats for the convenience of travellers; the day she comes from Saltcoats is Thursday. The freight is fixed to prevent impositions.

Glasgow Journal 12 March 1759

A Scene of Savage Sterility
Thomas Pennant, 1772

June 20. Most of the morning was passed in a dead calm: in the afternoon succeeded brisk gales, but from points not the most favorable, which occasioned frequent tacks in sight of port: in one broke our top-sail yard. During these variations of our course, had good opportunity of observing the composition of the isle of Arran: a series of vast mountains, running in ridges across the whole; their tops broken, serrated, or spiring; the summit of Goatfield rising far above the rest, and the sides of all sloping towards the water edge: a scene, at this distance, of savage sterility.

Another calm within two miles of land: take to the boat, and approach Loch-Ranza, a fine bay, at the N. end of the isle of Arran, where I land in the evening. The approach was magnificent: a fine bay in front, about a mile deep, having a ruined castle near the lower end, on a low far projecting neck of land, that forms another harbour, with a narrow passage; but within has three fathom of water, even at the lowest ebb. Beyond is a little plain

Lochranza Bay (from Pennant, A Tour, *1774)*

watered by a stream: and inhabited by the people of a small village. The whole is environed with a theatre of mountains; and in the back ground the serrated crags of Grianan-Athol soar above.

Visit the castle, which consists of two square parts united, built of red grit stone: in one room is a chimney piece, and fire place large enough to have roasted an ox: but now strewed with the shells of limpets, the hard fare of the poor people who occasionally take refuge here.

*

Am informed of a basking shark that had been harpooned some days before, and lay on the shore, on the opposite side of the bay. Cross over to take a view of a fish so rarely to be met with in other parts of Great Britain; and find it a monster, nothwithstanding it was much inferior in size to others that are sometimes taken; for there have been instances of their being from thirty-six to forty feet in length.

This was twenty-seven feet four inches long. The tail consisted of two unequal lobes: the upper five feet long: the lower three. The circumference of the body great: the skin cinereous and rough. The upper jaw much longer than the lower. The teeth minute, disposed in numbers along the jaws. The eyes placed at only fourteen inches distance from the tip of the nose. The apertures to the gills very long, and furnished with strainers of the substance of whalebone.

*

June 21. Procure horses, and (accompanied by Mr Lindsay, the minister) ride up the valley, cross the little river Ranza, and leave that and a corn-mill on the right. Ascend the steeps of the barren mountains, with precipices often on the one side of our path, of which our obstinate steeds preferred the very margin. See to the west the great crags of Grianan-Athol, with eagles soaring over their naked summits. Pass through woods of birch, small, weather-beaten and blasted: descend by Mac-farlane's Carn, cross the water of Sannocks, near the village of the same name: see a low monumental stone; keep along the eastern coast; hear a sermon preached beneath a tent formed of sails, on the beach; the congregation numerous, devout, and attentive, seated along the shore, forming a groupe picturesque and edifying.

Dine at the Corry; a small house, belonging to a gentleman of Airshire, who visits this place for the benefit of goats' whey.

Much barreness in the morning's ride: on the mountains were great masses of moor-stone; on the shore, mill-stone, and red grit-stone.

The ride is continued along the coast, beneath low cliffs, whose summits were cloathed with heath that hung from their margins, and seemed to distil showers of crystalline water from every leaf, the effect of the various springs above. Meet a flock of goats, skipping along the shore, attended by their herdsman: and observed them collecting, as they went, and chewing with great delight, the sea plants.

*

The quadrupeds are very few: only otters, wild cats, shrew mice, rabbets and bats: the stags which used to abound, are now reduced to about a dozen. The birds are eagles, hooded crows, wild pigeons, stares, black game, grous, ptarmigans, daws, green plovers and curlews. Mr Stuart in ascending Goat-field found the secondary feather of an eagle, white with a brown spot at the base, which seemed to belong to some unknown species. It may be remarked that the partridge at present inhabits this island, a proof of the advancement of agriculture.

The climate is very severe: for besides the violence of winds, the cold is very rigorous; and snow lay here in the vallies for thirteen weeks of the last winter. In summer the air is remarkably salubrious, and many invalids resort here on that account, and to drink the whey of goats' milk.

The principal disease here is the pleurisy: small-pox, measles and chincough visit the island once in seven or eight years. The practice of bleeding twice every year seems to have been intended as a preventative against the pleurisy: but it is now performed with the utmost regularity at spring and fall. The Duke of Hamilton keeps a surgeon in pay; who at those seasons makes a tour of the island. On notice of his approach, the inhabitants of each farm assemble in the open air; extend their arms; and are bled into a hole made in the ground, the common receptacle of the vital fluid.

*

The men are strong, tall and well made; all speak the Erse language, but the antient habit is entirely laid aside. Their diet is chiefly potatoes and meal; and during winter, some dried mutton or goat is added to their hard fare. A deep dejection appears in general through the countenances of all: no time can be spared for amusement of any kind; the whole being given for procuring the means of paying their rent; of laying in their fuel, or getting a scanty pittance of meat and cloathing.

*

The produce of the island is oats; of which about five thousand bolls, each equal to nine Winchester bushels, are sown: five hundred of beans, a few peas, and above a thousand bolls of potatoes, are annually set: notwithstanding this, five hundred bolls of oat-meal are annually imported to subsist the natives.

The live stock of the island is 3183 milch cows; 2000 cattle, from one to three years old; 1058 horses; 1500 sheep; and 500 goats: many of the two last are killed at Michaelmas, and dried for winter provision, or sold at Greenock.

*

The inhabitants in general are sober, religious and industrious: great part of the summer is employed in getting peat for fuel, the only kind in use here; or in building or repairing their houses, for the badness of the materials requires annual repairs: before and after harvest they are busied in the herring-fishery; and during winter the men make their herring-nets; while the women are employed in spinning their linnen and woollen yarn. The light they often use is that of lamps. From the beginning of February to the end of May, if the weather permits, they are engaged in laboring their ground: in autumn they burn a great quantity of fern, to make kelp. So that, excepting at new-year's-day, at marriages, or at the two or three fairs in the island, they have no leisure for any amusements: no wonder is there then at their depression of spirits.

*

June 22. Pass by the river Machrai, flowing through a rocky channel, which, in one part has worn thro' a rock, and left so contracted a gap at the top as to form a very easy step a-cross. Yet not long ago a poor woman in the attempt, after getting one foot over, was struck with such horror at the tremendous torrent beneath, that she remained for some hours in that attitude, not daring to bring her other foot over, till some kind passenger luckily came by, and assisted her out of her distress.

Arrive at Tormore, an extensive plain of good ground, but quite in a state of nature: seems formerly to have been cultivated, for there appear several vestiges of dikes, which might have served as boundaries. There is a tradition that in old times the shores were covered with woods; and this was the habitable part.

The want of trees in the internal part at present, and the kindly manner in which they grow about Brodic, favor this opinion.

On this plain are the remains of four circles, in a line, extending N.E. by S.W.; very few stones are standing to perfect the inclosure, but those are of a great size; and stand remote from each other. One is fifteen feet high and eleven in circumference. On the outside of these circles are two others: one differs from all I have seen, consisting of a double circle of stones and a mound within the lesser. Near these are the reliques of a stone chest, formed of five flat stones, the length of two yards in the inside: the lid or top is lost. In the middle of these repositories was placed the urn filled with the ashes of the dead to prevent its being broken; or to keep the earth from mixing with the burnt remains. In all probability there had been a cairn or heap of stones above....

At a small distance farther is a cairn of a most stupendous size, formed of great pebbles: which are preserved from being scattered about by a circle of large stones, that surround the whole base: a circumstance sometimes usual in these monumental heaps.

*

June 24. In the afternoon leave Brodic castle, cross a hill, descend by the village of Kilbride, and reach the harbour of Lamlash, where our vessel lay at anchor in the safest port in the universe, a port perfectly Virgilian:

Hic insula portum
Efficit objectu laterum.

A beautiful semilunar bay forms one part: while the lofty island of Lamlash extending before the mouth secures it from the east winds: leaving on each side a safe and easy entrance. The whole circumference is about nine miles; and the depth of the water is sufficient for the largest ships. This is the place of quarantine: at this time three merchantmen belonging to Glasgow lay here for that purpose, each with the guard boat astern.

In the bottom of the bay was a fine circular bason or pier now in ruins; the work of the good Dutchess of Hamilton.

Land on the island of Lamlash, a vast mountain in great part covered with heath; but has sufficient pasture and arable land to feed a few milch cows, sheep and goats, and to raise a little corn and a few potatoes.

Thomas Pennant (1726-1798) *A Tour in Scotland and Voyage to the Hebrides* (Chester, 1774)

Lamlash by W. Noel Johnson, 1894

A February Jaunt

[Mr Hutchison], 1783

Monday, 14th.—Seskin is one of the largest farms in the island, situated about seventeen miles from Bachelors' Hall [Shore House, near Whiting Bay]. In consequence of our yesterday's bargain [to go a jaunt] we (Mr McL., Mr D., Mr G., and self) set off about eleven o'clock. The day was rather warm than pleasant. A prodigious fog all round the coast permitted not the rays of the sun (though unclouded) to point out to us any land but our own barren mountains. Pladda—a low, flat-lying island, being nothing but a rabbit warren, unpeopled by the human race, situated, I suppose, about a league from Arran—was the only land detached from our own which Phoebus would condescend to render visible, and even that island was not so conspicuous as to enable me to form any proper idea of its dimensions. Mr Galt, turning very sick on the road, we thought it would be prudent to halt a little at Kildonan Castle, and endeavour to procure something for him; but money, fair words, promises, nor anything we could think of could procure for our patient so much as a drink of grog, a dram of whisky, or a draught of milk or whey. The proprietor of this farm has had a very long and cheap lease of it, and the fields are the most beautiful and the farthest forward that I have yet seen in the island. Prosperity seemed to smile upon the landlord, but he had a Nabal's heart and a Nabal's hand—it could not melt at the recital of distress, nor would so much as solace my friend with a cup of cold water. He never so much as asked us to participate of the shade which the very stones of the house could have imparted. Hospitality, these are not thy tabernacles! Blest are the habitations where thou residest! Looking round the fields, says Captain McLeish, 'They seem to have plenty, too.' Says Mr Dunlop, 'had they less they might perhaps be more liberal.' Says I, 'Fy upon them and their plenty!' Says Hugh Galt, 'Curse them and their plenty too.' 'May thistles,' says he, 'grow in place of wheat, and cockle in place of barley.' Well, there was no help for it, the day was advancing, and something we must determine on; Mr G. could not go forward. I proposed returning home with him, but he would not consent, so we with difficulty got a lad as a guide, whom we tipped with a shilling, who promised to carry him and his horse home, about three miles from this same Kildonan. Whenever we saw Mr Galt fairly on his way, we proceeded on ours, and came through many a wild and desolate place, till we arrived at Lagg. Here we dined on mutton ham (as hard as leather) and some eggs, for nothing else could this tavern afford us; but Mr McLeish, suspecting this would be the case, procured a fishing-rod, and in a few minutes brought in five excellent trout, which, with our ham and eggs, made a shift. After dinner we mounted our horses and proceeded to Seskin, the place where I am now writing, as both Mr

McL. and Mr D. are out. The rest of this day's transactions I shall write tomorrow if I can get it cleverly done.

Tuesday, 15th.—Yesternight Mr McLeish and I, walking round our landlord's farm in company with our said landlord, we discovered a long string of peat-diggers coming down from the moss, leaping and jumping like mad ones. Our landlord soon informed us they were his servants coming from the moors to supper, and that they usually had a dance after their work was over. Happy state, when the pleasures of life are not the business of life, but when they only serve to strengthen and encourage us in the performance of our duty. Our host was a Lowlander, his name Crawford, and could once shake his foot with the most agile, but age blunted his relish. No matter, the sweetness of his disposition was an encouraging circumstance to the young folks, who well knew it, and liked him well for it. After supper we heard the sprightly notes of a fiddle. Says Mr McLeish, 'Will you go and hear the music?' 'Yes,' says I, 'and see the dance too.' Accordingly we repaired to the great barn, where there were about ten or twelve fat, blooming country lassies walloping it away to the tune of 'Greig's Pipes'. Mr McLeish and I were soon accommodated with partners, and danced till we were tired, but were far eclipsed by the country lads, who had more kicks and flings in three sets than we had in fifty. So, having left something for them to drink, we left Seskin, and on our way by Monyquil and the String travelled many a weary step. Some hills were exceedingly steep, and we were obliged to alight and lead. Our view was often interrupted by exceeding high hills on each side the road, and when we got into a more open place our prospect was most ungraciously blocked up with thick mist and fog. Well, having drunk some grog at Brodick our business was to thank God for many things, to wit—1st, Our safe arrival without hurt or skaith of any kind; 2nd, Our meeting with only one Kildining all our life; 3rd, The happy meeting of about thirteen ladies and Mr Galt in perfect health, who, with a Mr Brice, two Mr Ferreys, and a Dr Shaw (brother to Miss Heely), served as guardships to the fleet, and saw them safe here, where we all dined together after the ladies had employed a little time at the toilet, as the riding six miles had shaken away the powder, which had no doubt perfumed the breeze, which those would relish who rode to the leeward. After dinner and a glass of wine, the ladies dropped off in pairs into another room, so we plied the glass pretty briskly; every now and then put in mind by the lady that it was turning late. Having seen them all mounted on their ponies, we followed. There were about 21 of us in the cavalcade. We rode pretty smart some part of the way, but stopping at Springbank a party drank tea there (at Mr McAlaster's). The rest of us proceeded to Lamlash, where we drank tea in two separate houses. We all mounted again, and arrived safe excepting one of the Miss Shaws (sister of Sir James Shaw, Baronet—the first Scotsman that was Lord Mayor of London—and mother of Sir John Shaw, Baronet) who fell twice off her horse, on which I soon reinstated her, being a bad and fearful rider. Says I—'Miss Peggy, if you'll ride double, my horse is strong;' but she declined it. So on we went, and arrived safe at Bachelors' Hall, and there took farewell of the ladies, as none of them could be prevailed upon to alight. The ladies were all dressed suitable to the occasion, and made a most capital appearance.

From 'Journal of a trip to Arran one hundred years ago. Written by a Glasgow merchant'. *Glasgow Evening Times* 1 January 1885

View of the Island of Arran
James Headrick, 1803

The Duke of Hamilton's factor is a justice of the peace, and baron-baillie within the island of Arran. From his decisions an appeal lies to the Sheriff of Bute at Rothsay. He may imprison a delinquent during forty-eight hours in Arran castle, until he can be sent to the county jail at Rothsay. Few crimes are committed; and capital offences are never heard of.

*

The people are remarkably pious and devout, without shewing any predilection for wild and extravagant notions of religion. Each parish has an established schoolmaster, agreeable to the law of Scotland; and there were formerly two or three schools established by the Society for Propagating Christian Knowledge, but they were withdrawn, from want of the requisite accommodations: which is much to be regretted.

*

Population: Males, 2377; Females, 2802; Total, 5179 (1801) ... How, then, shall we account for 425 females existing in the island of Arran, without help-mates? Many of the young men go to sea. Some never return; and those who do return, are never all assembled on the island at the same time. Hence, every enumeration of the males must fluctuate, and the number of females must always exceed that of males.

On the 6th and 7th of October 1803, the Depute-Lieutenants of the county found on the island 1500 men able to carry arms; and about 500 men liable to serve in the Militia and Army of Reserve. But such is the aversion of the people here to the land service, that they chose to pay the penalty; and only one or two could be prevailed upon to enter into the militia. The late Duke of Hamilton was so much beloved among them, on account of his kind condescension and extensive charities, that few of them speak of him with dry eyes. Yet, when he proposed to raise a regiment, he was able to prevail only on a very small number of them to join his colours; and these were enticed by extravagant bounties. Had he proposed to man a ship of the line, the people would have risen in mass.

Sea Fishing by W. Noel Johnson, 1894

The people have no other aversion to the naval service, than what is common to other seamen, viz. the superior wages given by merchants during war. Though not remarkable for gigantic stature, they are athletic and well shaped; and in our ships of war, are distinguished by prompt obedience, and orderly conduct.

This bent towards a seafaring life is not peculiar to the people of Arran; but is common to the inhabitants of all the islands and highlands that are contiguous to the sea. It marks the importance of putting the fisheries into a proper train of improvement.

I could not learn that the people here have any superstitions that are peculiar to them. The second sight has so long ceased to be known, that it now seems to be entirely forgotten. They seem still to entertain a faint belief in faires, witches, and ghosts; though even these seem to be rapidly falling into oblivion. Among the old men, there are numerous traditionary stories concerning Fiun and his heroes; though the poems have ceased to be repeated.

Mr Pennant...says, the people in Arran bleed, with the utmost regularity, at spring and fall.... I was well informed, that this story was told Mr Pennant in the way of joke; and that no such practice was ever known in Arran.

So far from the health of the people being treated in this butcher-like manner, the Dutchess of Hamilton established a salary to induce an able medical man to reside in the island. That office has always been ably filled; and by no one more so than by Mr Stoddart their present surgeon.

The small-pox only visit the island at distant intervals, being brought by people from the Mainland, and prove very fatal. Dr Stoddart has made several attempts to introduce the vaccine inoculation; but the matter, which was sent from Edinburgh, had lost its power, and did not take effect. Other diseases are few, and no way peculiar in their mode of operating.

Though most of the people understand English, many of them are bashful, and averse to speak it. The Gaelic appears to be a picturesque language, and to come home to their imaginations and feelings. But, in order to spread the knowledge of improvement, it would be desireable to have only one language. For this purpose, the clergy should gradually discontinue their discourses in Gaelic; and the schoolmasters should exert all their efforts to instruct the youth in a knowledge of English. This recommendation I would apply to the whole Highlands and Isles. Let us be one people, having one language, the same laws, and similar customs. In this way, and this alone, the power and prosperity of these kingdoms may be carried to an extent far beyond what they have yet attained.

The island of Lamlash is stretched across a spacious bay, which it defends from every storm. Its Gaelic name, when translated, is Holy Isle, because St Molios long chose it as the place of his residence.... I saw a cave on the western side of the island, in which he lived. I could not help remarking, that this Saint acquired his celebrity, when dirt, nastiness, and absurdity, formed the most prominent features of sanctity. Had he chosen a similar cave on the opposite side of this island, where no boat could approach him, and where people from Arran could not get to him without danger of breaking their bones among the loose fragments of rock, with which the beach is encumbered, we might have believed him to have retired from the haunts of men in downright earnest. But he chose a residence where the channel is narrowest, and most easily accessible from Arran, and within the bay, where vessels from all quarters would find safety. Hence his object must have been, not to retire from the world, but to draw the world after him; and I doubt not but in this cave he displayed more pride, vanity, and pomposity, than Diogenes in his tub, or Bonaparte while seating himself upon a throne.

*

The original breed [of horses] was very small; because, if a mare got a foal in the moors, she was allowed to rear it there, without assistance. Of late, breeding has much declined; and horses of a larger size are imported from Argyleshire, sometimes to cross with the natives, but more frequently for the purposes of labour. The late Duke endeavoured to improve the breed of this island, by importing stallions; by horse-races, and other premiums;—just as a predecessor of his established the Lanarkshire breed of horses, which, for labour, is unquestionably the best breed in the world. Those imported from Argyleshire, seem to have some of the Isle of Mull blood in them, derived from horses rescued from the wreck of the Spanish Armada. The original breed of Arran seems to have been derived from the same stock, and possesses all their good qualities, though under a diminutive form.

Such of these animals as are accustomed to the saddle, are docile and tractable in an extraordinary degree; patient of fatigue; endure hunger; and gratefully take any kind of food that is offered them. Their sureness of foot is most remarkable. They will scamper with you over loose fragments of rock, and down steep declivities covered by the same. In these cases, the judgment with which they choose their steps, and lift their feet over the larger blocks, is truly astonishing. In general, the slightest pull of the bridle will turn them any way you please. But there are cases, where they know they are right, and you are wrong; and if they should choose to walk along the very edge of an unfathomable precipice, it would be very dangerous to enter into a dispute with them. The result of the dispute would be, that the animal would take the road which it knew to be safest and best for itself; and your persevering in the argument would only endanger your being both thrown over the precipice.

The average size of horses here varies from about ten to fourteen hands high. Many of them are of size and strength sufficient to draw the two-horse plough, especially in such friable soils as abound in Arran. Were the requisites to be afterwards mentioned provided, and followed by judicious crossing, a breed might be reared here for the saddle superior to any in the world.

*

Serpents abound in Arran, and are thought to have multiplied since the birds of prey have been nearly extirpated. A species of hawk was described to me which preferred serpents to every other food. His method was, to seize the serpent by the tail, and carry him high in the air, swinging him so that he could not turn to bite; and, having dropped him upon a rock or stone, the serpent was so much stunned, that the hawk could descend and devour him in safety.

The serpents sometimes kill sheep, and convey to cows and horses, and even to men, a temporary lameness. The largest I saw were about three feet in length; but was told that many of them exceed four. I observed three species, clearly distinguished by their colour and spots; but as they are known to cast their skins, the people believe them to be all of one species, at different periods of their growth.

*

The Dutchess Ann, who seems to have been a woman of a strong mind, and far beyond the barbarous age in which she lived, first began the making of roads in Arran; and, as far as I could learn, excepting a few repairs, they never have been carried further than she left them. But, unfortunately, in her time, the proper lines of roads were not understood. In place of going round a hill, they went straight over its top. This may easily be accounted for from the ideas of those times. Wheel carriages, and their accommodation, did not enter into their thoughts, because they were hardly known. Roads on which people could ride without breaking their necks, and on which horses could carry a heavier load than they could on rugged precipices, was all that entered into their contemplation....

Arran requires a road all round her, and one from the head of Broddick Bay to Shiskin. In this extensive tract, great part of the road is already made by nature; and the rest, in most cases, only requires formation. In the track round the island, four difficult passes occur; but an observant eye can see a most easy road through them. No stone bridges exist in Arran; but a few are necessary; and nature has marked positions where a very small arch can be thrown from rock to rock, so situated as most effectually to render the road beneficial. In a few cases, gullies must be passed by a slope cut in the bank on each side.

In addition to these great lines, a few accommodation roads are necessary, to carry lime, or other manures, to improveable land; or to form communications between the cultivated land, and the proposed fishing stations on the sea-coast. These collateral roads may be executed when their necessity becomes obvious.

*

The climate here is considered as rather moist, though the opposite extreme prevailed while I sojourned in Arran. The gravelly and sandy soils need much rain; and it is only by frequent repetitions of moisture, that they can be brought to carry either corn or grass. They have another defect, that all the putrescent manures applied to them are mostly washed through the soil in one season; so that their application is like pouring water into a sieve. Clay marl, where it is near, has been recommended as the most powerful and most permanent corrective of the defects of these soils. Where it is remote, mossy or earthy composts may supply its place.

With regard to temperature, this island, and other places on the west coast, intersected by the sea, are not understood to be so warm in summer, nor so cold in winter, as other places on the same parallel, and of the same elevation, on the east. Nor does the medium temperature vary so much, as it does in the broadest part of the island, towards the south of England. Still less does the temperature vary so much, as it does on the same parallel, on the opposite continents of Europe and America.

In Arran, snow storms come from the north-east, or east. Having many mountains to cross before they reach this island, they are mostly exhausted before they arrive. Though snow sometimes lyes long on the granite mountains, it seldom remains a few hours on the low grounds; and, on the sea-shores, it is speedily dissolved.

This marks the adaptation of this island, and of other places similarly situated, for winter crops of every kind. Towards the south of Arran, where clay predominates, or the soil can be corrected by clay marl, wheat would thrive admirably. The soil and climate both admirably cooperate for raising turnips, yams, potatoes, and every species of roots; vetches, sown grasses, and every species of green crop. Nor is the climate and soil less favourable for improving the natural herbage which grows upon the mountains, or higher grounds, as already pointed out.

Rev. James Headrick *View of the Mineralogy, Agriculture, Manufactures and Fisheries of the Island of Arran, with Notices of Antiquities, and Suggestions for Improving the Agriculture and Fisheries of the Highlands and Islands of Scotland* (Edinburgh: Constable, 1807)

Bruce Steers for Arran

Sir Walter Scott, 1815

Now launched once more, the inland sea
They furrow with fair augury,
   And steer for Arran's isle;
The sun, ere yet he sunk behind
Ben-Ghoil, 'The Mountain of the Wind',
Gave his grim peaks a greeting kind,
   And bade Loch-Ranza smile.
Thither their destined course they drew;
It seemed the isle her Monarch knew,
So brilliant was the landward view,
   The ocean so serene;
Each puny wave in diamonds rolled
O'er the calm deep, where hues of gold
   With azure strove and green.
The hill, the vale, the tree, the tower,
Glowed with the tints of evening's hour,
   The beach was silver sheen;
The wind breathed soft as lover's sigh,
And, oft renewed, seemed oft to die,
   Oh, who, with speech of war and woes,
Would wish to break the soft repose
   Of such enchanting scene!
        *

On fair Loch-Ranza streamed the early day,
   Thin wreaths of cottage-smoke are upwards curled
From the lone hamlet, which her inland bay
   And circling mountains sever from the world.
And there the fisherman his sail unfurled,
   The goat-herd drove his kids to steep Ben-Ghoil,
Before the hut the dame her spindle twirled,
   Courting the sunbeam as she plied her toil,—
For, wake where'er he may, Man wakes to care and coil.

Sir Walter Scott (1771-1832) *The Lord of the Isles* (Edinburgh: Constable, 1815)

Various Instructive Phenomena
John Phillips, 1826

Aug. 6th (S) [1826]

Rising early I found the first view of Arran delightful. Brodick Bay is really very pretty and much ornamented by a few white Houses of resident Gentlemen especially toward the woody cliffs of Corygills. Some rough Glasgow bodies joined my breakfast table, who came to save money or gain health or avoid creditors.

Lamlash Church is 6 miles distant, and the showers kept me from going, though my pride was secretly touched when I found all the country people on the road regardless of the shaded sky. However I sat & finished my heaps of sketches. An eagle in the garden keeps bad company with a Hawk (*F. peregrinus*) whom he occasionally drives away from the fresh herrings— he moans a shrill whining tone.

After dinner I ascended Goatfield first by a road leading by cottages and through a Plantation of the Duke's and afterwards by a track across the wide heath. Red Sandstone appears up to the Plantation, Mica Slate overspread with Granite blocks underlays the Heath. The Pyramid above is Granite. The top became misty just as I was about to reach it, and prudence advised me to retire. The views from the side were grand & extensive. This Granite contains crystal-lined cavities.... In the quiet of this glorious evening my soul exulted in joy, to find that at last the opportunity had arrived when I might examine with my own eyes unprejudiced & at leisure the various instructive Phenomena for which this Island is deservedly celebrated.

Aug. 7.

… Lamlash is a fine bay, surrounded by sloping Hills, is newly built, and being tolerably regular and very white looks respectable, a small pier as at Brodick serves a few fishing Vessels. It has a post-office and a well-frequented Kirk. Few visitors stop here. A Packet 3 days a week to Saltcoats.

Returning to Brodick I climbed Dunfion, if that be so named which is the highest point between Brodick and Lamlash. Halfway up I found a sort of Porphyry and perhaps Sandstone above. The summit is Greenstone. It commands a fine view out over the water where a Steam Packet is seen coming from Ardrossan to Lamlash with a pleasure-party. We see beyond Corry to the North and Whiting Bay to the South. Brodick & Lamlash with their rival bays and Inns are both beneath our eye. Holy Isle is above us.

John Phillips (1800-1874) *Tour Round Scotland* (MS. in Mitchell Library)

Thou Majestic Arran

Rev. David Landsborough (1828)

There plies the smoking steam-boat, which, with power
Like his whose magic touch and wizard skill
Keeps thus in close, but sweetest bondage bound,
Castle, and town, and sea, and mountain wild;—
Brings to our homes what late were foreign lands;
And binds with happy tie to kindred shore
Islands which floated long in lonely pride,
Amidst the waters of the western main.
And thou majestic ARRAN! dearest far
Of all the isles, on which the setting sun
In golden glory smiles; Queen of the West,
And Daughter of the Waves! there art thou too,
Rearing aloft thy proud aerial brow,
Claiming the homage of admiring lands,
O'er a wide range of tributary shores.

Thee much I love; partly I wot, because
I've oft explored thy glens and tangled brakes,
Where every bank blooms with the primrose pale,
And drooping hyacinth; or where amidst
Her ensiformal leaves, on stately stem,
Sweet *Epipactis*, rarest of thy plants,
Builds up her pyramid of snowy gems.—

Thee much I love; because I've often climbed
Thy mountains brown, and scaled their towering peaks,
Where high 'midst rocky battlements sublime,
Flora conceals from reach of vulgar gaze,
The loveliest of her fair, but fleeting race.—
And whence in panoramic view beheld
Far as the eye can reach are Scotia's Isles;
And intervening seas; and mountains blue;
And fertile vales, far as Edina's towers.
Whence, too, are seen in varied shades and hues,
Erin's green shores; and Mona's distant hills;
And merry England's coast; like summer clouds,
Softly commingling with the azure sky.—

*

But let us now forsake these airy heights,
These peaks pyramidal of mountains wild.
Rugged as yet has been our path, and steep;
But softer, sweeter scenes await us now,

25

While we perambulate with easy step,
The well-sunned scenes which smile upon the sea.
　　To Brodwick, then, our sloping path directs;
To Brodwick,—best beheld,—not from the heights,—
But from the bosom of her lovely bay,
Or from the verdant villa-studded shore.
See amidst trees embosomed which have braved
The fiercely rushing blasts of hundred years,
Her ducal tower; the scene indeed adorning.
But by the scene, itself still more adorned.
Trace thence Glen-rosa, as like Beauty coy
Softly retiring with most winning grace,
She winds her way amidst romantic hills,
Till lost in deepest, wildest solitudes,
She hides herself from the admiring eye.
Mark, too, the heath-clad heights and peaks sublime
Which this famed bay in Alpine pride surmount;—
Survey the whole;—and if unmoved you look,
Then turn your eyes from Nature's fairest scenes;
For to the grand and sweet and beautiful
Your soul is blind, your heart is dead and cold.
　　But if to Nature's loveliness alive;—
Turn your exploring eyes to sweet LAMLASH:
And though her charms are of a different kind,
'Tis such a difference as in sisters fair
Of graceful family, well pleased we find.
View then the Bay by the majestic cone
Of HOLY ISLE, secure and peaceful made....
　　And pleasant sight it is to view this Bay,
When after days of elemental strife
A morning blithe ensues. Then all is joy
And cheerfulness throughout the crowded Loch.
Then all the vessels tight, that lately lay
Close reefed and moored, prepare for issuing forth,
To stem, if *home* is sought,—the winding Clyde;
If foreign shores,—to plow the tolling main.
Then the spread canvass courts the swelling breeze;
And from each busy deck the sailors' voice
Is heard in merry cheerings; merrier far
From recollection of the recent storm.
　　　　　　　　*

　　The evening sun shone on the splendid scene,
Gilding the mellow summits of the peaks,
When Cìoch-na-h-ighinn first in grandeur rose,

26

Like stateliest daughter of the Anakim,
In virgin dignity and native grace.
Then Ceum-na-caillich burst upon our view,
Like some vast pyramid in days of yore,
By superhuman power here piled on high.
Next Cir-mhòr, in pectinated pride
And rugged grandeur, reared his massy crest.
Then Sue-Ergus, like a giant huge,
Though long invincible, now laid supine,
And looking up as suppliant to the skies.
    How truly wonderful these alpine heights!
Who can their hidden history unfold?
Who tell their origin? Is what we see
The mighty fragment of a nobler world
Than that which we inhabit? Or remains
Of ancient temple, where a race of men
More potent than the mightiest now on earth,
Met to adore the only Power that could
A temple so magnificent uprear?
Or formed these airy peaks which rise around
An amphitheatre surpassing far
Aught that the richest potentates and kings,
In all the plenitude of wealth and power,
E'er tried to raise? Do not these pinnacles
Which lightly shoot into the middle air,
In Fancy's eye no slight resemblance bear
To ruined pillars of colossal form;—
To columns of a nobler colonnade
Than Grecian architecture ever reared?
    But rest not satisfied with having seen
From Sannox-bay these bold and striking peaks.
Land near that house of God; the Glen pervade;
Stop not till Ceum-na-caillich's highest cliffs
Thou'st bravely scaled, and ere the evening close,
Return to linger round the lovely bay.
Lovest thou solitude 'midst scenes sublime?
Here take thy fill; for having left the bay,
And the soft landscape close upon the shore,
A grander, wilder, lonelier Highland glen
Thou nowhere canst behold. The glen to trace,
To mount the towering summits, and return,
Hours of laborious effort will require;
Yet all the while, nor glimpse of face divine,
Nor human habitation, wilt thou see.

Yet think not tenantless this noble glen.
Here with wild note the wheeling plovers rise;
There whirring spring the snowy ptarmigan,
And eke the blackcock bold on glossy wing.
High 'mong the cliffs abrupt of Kier-vore
The screaming eagle flutters o'er her nest,
And stirreth up her young. And see where hang
From Kiech-na-hean's peak the shaggy goats,
Though steep as obelisk it mounts on high.
Nay, ere you leave the glen, be not surprised
Though the red deer start from his humble lair
'Mong the deep purple heath, and bound away
In all his branching honours o'er the heights,
And down Glen-rosa; or across the wilds
Which to Ben-vaaran lead. His stately step,
His graceful motions, how can you behold
And not confess within your raptured heart
Feelings at once delightful and sublime.
You honour him as monarch of the glen;
As of the ancient stock which flourished there,
When royal BRUCE, and his most faithful friends,
Traversed with hound and horn these rugged wolds,
Rousing the sleeping echoes of Ben-ghoil;—
Waging, with arrows winged, unequal war
With the forefathers of this antlered chief.

Rev. David Landsborough (1779-1854) *Arran: A Poem. In Six Cantos* (Edinburgh: Blackwood, 1828)

The Saddle and Cir-Mhor by W. Noel Johnson, 1894

'Was There a Bonnier Sight'

John Wilson, 1829

TICKLER. From a kingdom, we have already sunk into a province; let the thing go on much longer, and from a province we shall fall to a colony—one of 'the dominions thereunto belonging!' They are knocking our old entail law to pieces as fast as they can, and the English capitalists and our Glossins between them, will, before many days pass, have the soil to themselves—unless something be done—and I for one shall do *mon possible*.

SHEPHERD. Weel, if the gentry lose the land, the Highland anes at ony rate, it will be the Lord's righteous judgment on them for having dispossessed the people before them. Ah! wae's me—I hear the Duke of Hamilton's cottars are a' gaun away, man and mither's son, frae the Isle o' Arran. Pity on us! was there a bonnier sight in the warld, than to sail by yon green shores on a braw summer's evening, and see the smoke risin' frae the puir bodies' bit shielings, ilk ane wi' its peatstack and its twa three auld donnerd pines, or saughs, or elms, sugh-sughin' owre the thack in the gloamin' breeze?

John Wilson (1785-1854) *Noctes Ambrosianae* No. XLVI *Blackwood's Magazine* September 1829

On the Frith of Clyde (in a Steamboat)

William Wordsworth, 1833

Arran! a single-crested Tenerife,
A St Helena next—in shape and hue,
Varying her crowded peaks and ridges blue;
Who but must covet a cloud-seat, or skiff
Built for the air, or winged Hippogriff?
That he might fly, where no one could pursue,
From this dull Monster and her sooty crew;
And, as a God, light on thy topmost cliff.
Impotent wish! which reason would despise
If the mind knew no union of extremes,
No natural bond between the boldest schemes
Ambition frames and heart-humilities.

Beneath stern mountains many a soft vale lies,
And lofty springs give birth to lowly streams.

William Wordsworth (1770-1850) Itinerary poems of 1833 *The Poems* edited by Thomas Hutchinson (London: Oxford University Press, 1911)

The People of Arran
John Paterson, 1834

In moral character the people of Arran resemble those of the inhabitants of other Highland districts. They are hospitable among themselves and to strangers. They are more confiding in each other than is altogether prudent. The money and other property of the more fortunate among them are freely lent to those in need, often when there is but a slight prospect of repayment. To their aged and infirm relations they are generally kind and dutiful, and scarcely any are ever allowed to beg their bread. The poor are supported by the collections made at the church doors, aided by small pensions given by the family of Hamilton, principally to old women.

The people of Arran may be justly described as a religious community. They have generally a competent knowledge of the leading principles of Christianity, mixed, however, with many superstitions, and not a little of what better informed people call fanaticism. Although generally honest in their dealings with one another, they frequently, like the Jews, think it no crime to get as much as they can from strangers, or those in a situation above them in rank. Many also feel an undue jealousy of the conduct and intentions of their superiors, and discover a cunning and art in prosecuting their little objects with those who they think can further them, that are often laughable, and sometimes shew considerable knowledge of human nature.

They generally marry young, often when they have provided but little with which to begin house-keeping. They are very frugal, live on the coarsest food, and often contrive to rear healthy families on means which appear very inadequate. Very few illegitimate children are born in the island; and although there are some customs among the young men and women that may appear inimical to chastity, self-control is certainly very much practised. They generally make good husbands and wives, and affectionate parents, very sober and attentive to their religious duties. So far as recollected, there is not a single native who can with justice be called a drunkard. Although the women perform a considerable portion of the out-door work in harvest and at peat-cutting time, they cannot be called drudges to the men. Formerly the people were much addicted to litigation, but there is now a marked improvement in this respect, very few cases being brought before the magistrates. Illicit distillation, which prevailed to a great extent, has now nearly altogether disappeared.

The personal appearance of the Arran people is not such as we are accustomed to consider very good. They are generally short, strongly made, with coarse irregular features and high cheek-bones, the feet and limbs, especially of the females, very clumsy, the former being large and flat, the ankles thick, and the heel projecting considerably beyond the limb. Black is the prevailing colour of the hair. They are very polite and insinuating in their address, and rarely exhibit those awkward and boorish manners so common on the mainland. To their superiors they shew great respect, so much so, indeed, that it is sometimes annoying. Yet, though even a little in excess, such conduct is more pleasant to witness than the very reverse, so often to be met with in the more improved parts of the kingdom.

Even so late as seventeen years ago, the females, when at church, were coarsely dressed, often in home-made clothes; the unmarried with a ribbon or band on the head, the married with a close cap. Now, the young women dress in calicoes and muslins, some of them in silks, and wear straw or Leghorn bonnets. The matrons still prefer the close cap.

In this district, the people are exceedingly superstitious. They firmly believe in the power of the 'evil eye', in apparitions of many different kinds, and in charms for healing diseases. Few dare to travel alone at night for fear of ghosts, and they are terribly in dread of a kind of spirit which they call the 'white sack', which is said to be in fact a full white sack rolling on the ground!

John Paterson 'Account of the Island of Arran' (1834) *Prize Essays and Transactions of the Highland and Agricultural Society of Scotland*, Vol.XI (Edinburgh and London: Blackwood and Cadell, 1837)

Summers by the Sea
Elizabeth King, 1834

In the beginning of May, 183[4], we went to a cottage which we had taken for the summer at Invercloy in Arran. By this time my strength was so gone that I had to be carried down to Aunt Graham's carriage, and then lifted on board the steamer, and laid on a bed prepared for me. The vessel was the 'Glenalbin', a Glasgow and Londonderry boat, which our father had engaged to put in to Invercloy and drop us there, as no steamboats were plying to Arran at the time. On our arrival, I was carried ashore to the little Brodick

Inn, and next day conveyed to our own cottage, lying on a mattress spread on a country cart. It was headaches that I suffered from, and I do not think I should have been so weak and ill but for the treatment to which I had been subjected, being bled at least once a fortnight with leeches, and often blistered on the back of my neck. It was wonderful how quickly my strength now came back. In a few weeks I was able to walk a mile or two, and my brothers often trundled me in a wheelbarrow along a smooth greensward that bordered the shore; and so enabled me to reach further distances than would otherwise have been possible at first. ([Letter of] June 6, 1834: 'We have no conveniences. We cannot even get a little salt or pepper, or a little flour, without sending to Saltcoats. Our bread comes from Saltcoats, and it is excellent. The eggs were fourpence a dozen, but they are now fourpence-halfpenny. The milk is very fine, but not a bit of tolerable butter is to be had. Butcher meat is seldom to be had, but we have never felt the want of it yet. We had a quarter of veal at fourpence per pound, which served us for a week with the assistance of eggs.')

On Sunday mornings the family went, in an open cart of the country, seated with rough benches and straw, across from Brodick to Lamlash, where was the parish church—the only one in the island. It happened one Sunday that there was a revival service, and the congregation grew much excited, uttering loud exclamations and groans; and at last some of the old women began to give vent to their feelings by tossing their Bibles in the air. This tickled Willie's sense of humour, and he shook with smothered laughter, which started all the other boys laughing too. Our pew was close under the pulpit in full view of the preacher, who, looking down, administered a grave rebuke. The smothered laughter then exploded, and the minister, pointing his finger at the ringleader, exclaimed, 'Ye'll no lach when ye're in hell!' This was too much: and Willie rolled clean over on to the floor. For some reason or other our father was not with us that day, and I was in charge of the party. Crimson with shame, I bustled them all out of the church as quickly as I could.

The island at that time seemed very remote and inaccessible, yet we found plenty of agreeable society ready to welcome us. Dr Meikleham, Professor of Natural Philosophy, whom William afterwards succeeded, had a house quite near; and we had much friendly intercourse with him and his family. He was a good-natured, fat, little hunchback, with a very red face; and he had a fat, little, curly-haired black dog called Jura, that always toddled beside him. He had had the creature for many years, and when she died a year or two later, he lamented her as a lost friend. His daughter was a short, stout, benevolent lady, who was extremely kind to us. She often lent me her riding horse, on which, led by Jamie Brown, I accompanied our father and the others in their longer walks. Besides the Professor and his daughter, there were three boys in the family, a little older than any of my brothers, and they used to go out boating together.

We had our cottage from Captain Fullarton, who was joint-proprietor of the island with the Duke of Hamilton, and had the title deeds of his property from Robert Bruce, signed by his own royal hand. Both Captain and Mrs Fullarton bestowed much kindness upon us, and often invited us to their nice old house up Glen Cloy to meet their friends. The Duke of Hamilton sometimes called and had long talks with our father. He was anxious to persuade Captain Fullarton to sell his estate to him, that he might become sole lord of the island; but the Captain would not consent to part with the lands so long held by his forefathers. I think it would have been mean-spirited had he sold such a birthright. My father dined at the Castle once at any rate, and afterwards he used now and then to go out to Hamilton and dine at the palace. Once when the Duke came to see us in Arran he had on tartan trousers, and to our great surprise we saw holes in the knees. He was very peculiar; for instance, he had his coffin made, and lay down in it every day when at home to accustom himself to the idea of death; and he had his mausoleum built in view of the windows of Hamilton Palace.

We remained in our summer quarters till about the middle of October. The Londonderry steamer had taken us down in the beginning of May, and my father wrote requesting that it should put in to take us home. We had all packed and ready; but very tempestuous weather intervened, and we were storm-stayed for about ten days in a most uncomfortable condition, hoping to get off each day, and afraid to unpack lest the boat should suddenly appear. While the rain streamed down the window panes and the wind howled without, we were reduced to seek entertainment in the pages of an old newspaper by reading them in a new fashion—not down the columns but straight across the page from left to right—and laughing, as merry young people can laugh, at the utter nonsense thus produced.

At last on a Saturday afternoon the wind lulled and the sun shone; and the captain of one of Her Majesty's revenue cutters, lying in the bay, kindly offered to take us across to Ardrossan. He sent one of his boats with half a dozen bluejackets to row us out to the vessel, and we greatly enjoyed the rapid rowing as well as the sail across the Firth in the cutter. We spent Sunday in a hotel, which we thought delightful, and on Monday we went up to Glasgow in one of the regular coasting steamers. And when the 'Glenalbin' put in at Brodick Bay the birds were all flown.

Elizabeth King *Lord Kelvin's Early Home* (London: Macmillan, 1909)

Sketches of Arran

Lord Teignmouth, 1836

The Alpine character of the scene was heightened by a recent fall of snow, which lay four inches deep on the mountains, and by passing snow-storms, which the north-wind, rising at noon, according to the prediction of the guide, drove furiously before it, gradually scattering the dense array of clouds which enveloped the horizon, and discovering in all its extent a magnificent panoramic prospect, embracing the coast of Ireland, Sanda, Cantyre, Isla, the paps of Jura—now capped with snow,—Mull, Ben Cruachan, the mountains of Glencoe and Ben Lomond, the winding shores of Loch Fine and the Clyde, Bute and its Kyle, the Cumbrays, Ayrshire, Ailsa, and the Mull of Galloway, encircling the majestic pedestal on which we stood.

A pass between Ben Noosh and the Comb conducts to Goatfell. An affecting circumstance lately occurred on the latter mountain. The wife of a small farmer, of Thundergay, on the western shore of Arran, had set out from home with the intention of carrying a blanket to her son, who had just married and resided at Brodick, as a wedding present. She mistook her route and climbed a steep pass, by which, but for an unhappy accident, she might, though with toil, have reached her destination. Her son, not seeing her, concluded she had deferred her visit; and at her home it was supposed that she was safely lodged under her son's roof. A fortnight elapsed before her absence was discovered; and she was at length found dead at the highest point of the pass, wrapped in the bridal blanket, in which, as the guide observed, she had composed herself, that she might die decently, her head leaning on her hand, holding a piece of bread. The cause of her catastrophe was the fracture of her thigh-bone.

Goatfell is on this side steep and sandy, and channelled by torrents. We had just reached the ridge which forms the summit of the mountain, the highest point of which is 2,945 feet, when a whirlwind of snow on one of the peaks to windward indicated the approach of a blast which at once prostrated us; and we remained clinging to the rocks for some minutes. My guide stood aghast for some time after it had passed, and then broke his silence by a characteristic observation, 'I never saw the like before; I am sure that all the wind in the glen had gathered up to go thegither through that slap (pass).'

*

The produce of Arran has been doubled during the last fourteen years, by the improvement of cultivation, which dates from that period, and which has taken place chiefly on the enlargement of farms. Much barley is exported to Campbeltown to supply the distilleries, the only distillery erected in Arran having been disused. The inferiority of the cattle of this island is ascribed to small farms and insufficient feeding; the average rental of farms being from 10*l*. to 30*l*., with the exception of some few which reach to 100*l*. 200*l*. and 300*l*. The farmers are consequently, in general, little above the level of common labourers. The Duke encourages the reclamation of moorland by bounties. I saw a tract formerly let to six people, who cultivated very little of it, and grazed the rest. It was divided at the period of general improvement into twelve allotments, each of which now pays 5*l*. to 10*l*. rent.

The neighbourhood of Glasgow, and the visits of strangers, have rendered the farm-houses and cottages of Arran, in general, superior to those of Cantyre. But the same absurd system obtains here, as in some other parts of the Highlands, of repairing windows with wood, pane by pane, till the gradual extinction of light renders necessary the use of glass. The people appear to have taken a hint from the modern mode of operating for the cataract, by deferring the removal of the film till the sight of both eyes is perfectly extinguished.

The naval and merchant service has afforded a continual resource to the people of Arran: nearly 200 persons lately took their departure to America, from Glen Sannox, on its being laid under sheep; the Duke of Hamilton having allotted to each family a portion of land, obtained from the government, together with the sum of 5*l*.

*

The disposition of the people of Arran is strongly religious. Domestic worship, which is by no means general in Cantyre, is almost universal amongst them, and the Scriptures are so generally diffused amongst them, that they are fastidious in the choice of editions. They are, in general, well instructed, and possess, as in the Lowlands, small libraries of religious books, which they lend to one another. The following is a sample of the books which I found in the cottage of an old sailor—*Calvin's Institutes, Henry's Bible, Sermons by the Commentators,* (C.W. Guthrie, Bruce, Welwood, R. Cameron, D. Cargill, A. Pendon, A. Shield) and *Boston's Fourfold State.* He conversed on the prophetical parts of Scripture, and referred more especially to the prophecies of the Old Scottish divines, expressing his persuasion that good men were endowed with the gift of prophecy, though they could not exactly fix the period at which their predictions would be verified.

The religious habits of the people are promoted by their assemblage at each other's houses, for religious exercises, consisting of singing, reading, expositions, and addresses. As these meetings are frequent and protracted, they occasionally become polemical, and afford scope for the ostentatious display of learning, intellectual gladiatorship, fanaticism, and repugnance to church-government and discipline. There are also lay preachers. I accidentally became acquainted with the head of these, an old man named Mackinnon, who is considered the patriarch of Arran. He had been very much reduced in his circumstances, by the transfer of his farm to other

35

hands, and occupied a small cottage and piece of land. He was formerly wont to preach in a large cave, on the west-coast of the island, called the King's Cove, as having harboured Robert Bruce for some days before he raised his standard. On one occasion, a woman having fallen into convulsions,—for it is the prevailing notion among the more fanatical of the people of Arran, as among the old Wesleyans, and present Ranters, that some external bodily sign or convulsive emotion is a necessary sign of true repentance,—Mackinnon is said to have coolly observed, after they had ceased, 'poor thing, what a struggle she had with the devil.' Most of these preachers object to education, or, as they designate it, unsanctified learning in the clergy; making it the subject of animadversion in their discourses. In compliance with the prejudices of his parishioners a minister of one of the parishes of Arran was lately compelled to part with his pianoforte, a *whistling manse* being, it must be presumed, next akin to a *whistling kirk*.

*

Dissent has been almost extinguished by the removal of the inhabitants of Glen Sannox, to whom it was chiefly confined.

The morals of the people of Arran are well reported of; they are too poor to purchase spirits, and make very general use of tea: and it is the custom to prepare it for every visitor, as the dram was offered formerly; this ceremony is sometimes repeated three or four times in the day, and is said to be productive of idleness. The chief resource of the inhabitants is tobacco.

John Shore, Lord Teignmouth (1751-1834) *Sketches of the Coasts and Islands of Scotland* (London: John Parker, 1836)

The Ascent of Goatfell
Elvira Anna Phipps, 1840

...we attempted the ascent of Goatfell, no easy task, nor is it easy to recount the adventures of that day of excessive fatigue, and unparalleled enjoyment. The morning proved bright without a single cloud, and every object however distant was distinctly visible. The early part of the journey was a mere toiling up hills of heather. The mountains of granite before us began to look very formidable, and something whispered, is it possible that we shall ever stand upon that gigantic peak that seems to reach the sky! However our good old guide noticed these desponding thoughts, and immediately began to occupy our minds otherwise, that we might be less sensible of the fatigues we were undergoing. By the bye, I have omitted to give my reader a formal introduction to this personage... Sandy Crawford is his name, and he has been the only guide to Goatfell for the last fourteen years.

I soon perceived much originality of character about him. He gave me the whole history of his family, and entered minutely into the system of education he had pursued with his children; and the simplicity with which he described their daily meetings to read the Scriptures together, and the unsophisticated, pious strain of his discourse, pleased me not a little. He seemed quite a stranger to artifice, no one could suspect him of attempting to get up an effect in order to work upon our sympathies. In reply to his own stock of information, which was pretty considerable, allowing for his having lived all his life upon this island—he required from me many details concerning England, more especially respecting the Queen. He was very anxious to know whether the Queen would be likely to visit Arran—what the Queen would give a body like him if he took the trouble of travelling all the way to London to see her—and whether there were any good inns to be found in London, where a body like him could be comfortable—he had heard that the inns there were very bad, and full of noisy, drunken men, and as he was very frugal in his own habits, this would not suit him at all. He dwelt some time upon the fact that the Queen was no *Romanist*, that she would forfeit her crown if she ever became such. I perceived also that his mind was strongly tinctured with predestinarian notions. On one occasion, we came to the edge of a frightful precipice, and he told me that a few years ago, a gentleman was killed there. He was overtaken by a fog, the wind had blown off his hat, and in running after it, he did not perceive he was on the brink of a preceipice, and he fell over, and was dashed to atoms. His daughter was on a pony near the spot at the time.

Seeing how much I was affected by this melancholy event, Sandy said to me—'Ah! lady, that was the death he was to die, and he could not avoid it.'

Elvira Anna Phipps *Memorials of Clutha: or, Pencillings on the Clyde* (London: C. Armand, for the author, 1841)

Corrie an Lachan
Andrew Ramsay, 1841

This little sheet of water is by far the most picturesque of all the lochs of Arran, and is situated deep in a hollow, called Corrie an Lachan. The place is perfectly lonely; not a tree is near; and except the brown heath on its margin, and a few stunted rushes by the brook, the surrounding hills are almost bare of vegetation. The water is dark and deep, and the stormy blasts of the mountain never reach its still and unruffled surface. From its edge, on all sides but that towards the sea, rise the naked hills, whose sides are either formed of massive granite blocks, which, though surely yielding to

Corrie an Lachan by A.C. Ramsay, 1841

decay, yet offer a stronger resistance to the destroying influences of time than the softer portions of the mountain, where the decomposing rock may almost be seen slowly crumbling away.

Andrew Crombie Ramsay (1814-1891) *The Geology of the Island of Arran from Original Survey* (Glasgow: Richard Griffin, 1841)

A Taste for the Tops of Hills
Henry, Lord Cockburn, 1842

Ardrossan, Friday, 9th September 1842, 7 A.M.—Lord Mackenzie has gone to Inveraray, and we don't begin at Glasgow till Thursday next, the 15th, and my object in coming here is to get over to Arran, where I have never been, and to pass some days in its solitudes. But the window I am writing at looks across the water, and Arran is invisible, the waves surly, and the air showery. My contemptible stomach almost turns at the look of it, and is not made steadier by the pitching of a sloop a mile or two out. So my long desire to be in Glen Sannox, or on the top of Goatfell, may probably not be gratified today.

*

Brodick Inn, Sunday Morning, 11th September 1842.—Yesterday was so little bad that we resolved to tempt the deep. But we lost Maitland, for just before embarking, a letter from Mrs Cockburn, who is in Edinburgh, announced the death of her and Mrs Maitland's only surviving brother. The event was expected, and in his wretched and incurable state of suffering not to be deplored. It induced Maitland, however, to go to Edinburgh to give directions, and made his wife stay behind. So Helen, George, and James Maitland, Henry Davidson, my Elizabeth and Francis, and myself came here.

We left Ardrossan at ten. I took the precaution of lying down flat on the deck and shutting my eyes, from the very first moment of going on board till we reached Brodick, with the effect, which I had experienced before, of a total exemption from sickness. The voyage is about an hour and a half long.

The clouds said No, to our question whether we should ascend Goatfell. So George Maitland, H. Davidson, and I proceeded and explored Glenrosie, the outlet of which is within a mile of this, and the valley not above three or four miles long. There is, fortunately, no road, and the upper part is so stony and so cut into holes by streams, that it makes rather a severe scramble. But it is a valley well worth passing a day in. All gushing with the clearest water tumbling over granite; deep sides, browned with chocolate-coloured autumn fern, many dark rocky peaks, and the upper end enclosed by as striking an assemblage of black and picturesque precipitous mountain-tops as is often to be seen.

Not wishing to return the same way, we climbed to the top of the range which forms the left boundary of the valley, and came home *over* it instead of *round* it. It was a tough pull, and took us apparently more than half up Goatfell. The prospect was extensive, but there was too much islandless sea.

On the way home Davidson and I went into Brodick Castle,—a strong thing, with antiquity, site, and trees, sufficient to have enabled its noble owner, if he had chosen to spare a little of the gilding he has wasted on the weavers of Hamilton, to have easily made it a fine place. The gardener, who took us to the top of the house, when we asked him to point out the way to the top of the hill, did so, but added, with something like a boast, that though he had been living at its base for sixty years, he had never once attempted to ascend it.

I have walked this morning to the opposite (or south) side of the bay. It is by far the best of the two, at least when warmed, as it was an hour ago, by the morning sun, and in full prospect of the castle rising over its respectable wood, and of the craggy summits of Goatfell. Every one of the neat white cottages that are scattered about round the whole bay is let to people who come here in summer for health or idleness, and it was delightful to see so many comfortable breakfasts laid out, in small, but very clean, well-papered, cottage rooms. The church bell sounded, I don't know why, as I was told that there was to be no service, but its sound added greatly to the charm of the tranquil scene. The day is balmy, clear, and calm.

Brodick Inn, Monday, 8 A.M., 12th September 1842.—The guides don't practise their profession upon Sunday, even when there is no service, and therefore practised their established pious fraud, of assuring us that yesterday would be a bad day, but this a good one. We therefore got a boy with two horses, on which we put Helen and Elizabeth, and having packed a little refreshment into a basket, we all set out on the ascent. The horses could only get about half-way up. The girls then dismounted, and tried their own proper muscles. But Helen soon failed, and was established on the lee-side of a rock till our return. Elizabeth went to the very top. After lingering there a long while, we picked up the one we had left, recreated ourselves out of the basket, put the ladies on their beasts, and were all safe here in about five and a half hours from our setting out, which had been about eleven.

The guides proved so far right, that soon after our reaching the top, we, and all our world, were covered with mist. But it did not come on till after we had seen everything, and cleared off three or four times. And it was only the Argyleshire side that it ever entirely hid, leaving Clyde almost constantly bright. It was not therefore a *perfect* day for Goatfell, but it was not a *very bad* one. We saw everything, but only not long, or steadily, enough. With the exception of this partial misfortune on the *summit*, the whole ascent and descent were absolutely perfect, and the day, in every respect, was delicious.

In point of mere climbing, the ascent, except over a few rocks near the top, is not at all formidable. A mule could go to the very summit.

I have a taste for the tops of hills; but making allowance for this failing, it is certainly well worth the while even of a lover of flat ground, to mount Goatfell. It gives him a splendid prospect, both of land and water. Nature has rarely been more fortunate. The elevation of nearly 3,000 feet of granite, in an island, placed in the wide bay between Argyle on the west, and Renfrewshire and Ayrshire on the east, and near the openings of Loch Fyne and the Firth of Clyde; from which all the adjacent seas, and firths, and lochs, and sounds, and mountains, and islands are distinctly visible, was one of her happiest achievements.

I have been on a good many Scotch hills; but the competitors for the first prize are only four; Ben Lomond, Goatfell, Demyet, and Swanston (but neither this nor Cape Law is the correct name), the eastmost of the Pentlands. The claim of Ben Lomond rests chiefly on the stupendous mass of boiling mountains behind it. In point of *beauty* Demyet is perhaps to be preferred, because it is very low, and holds a delightful district of striking objects, particularly Stirling, within its eye. Goatfell bids defiance to them all, in the bright and varied splendour of its many, and islanded waters, contrasted with the hard and generally dark Argyleshire

View from Summit of Goatfell by J.D. Harding

peaks, by which these waters seem to be guarded and looked upon. But still, considering the beauty of Edinburgh, and the dignity imparted to scenery by objects of importance, I am rather inclined to give the palm to that Pentland.

For *prospects*, Ben Lawers, Ben Ledi, Ben More, and Ben Nevis, are to be altogether discounted. Ben Nevis however, has an indisputable superiority of interest, of a different kind to every other height in the British Islands. No other mountain is nearly so grand *in itself*....

This is another beautiful day, but not for the hill-top, and I rejoice that we did not wait for it yesterday.

Brodick Inn, Monday Night, 12th September 1842.—This forenoon was given to Glen Sannox. Elizabeth, Eliza Maitland (who came over this morning from Ardrossan with my daughter Jane), H. Davidson, George Maitland, and I, got in, and upon, a car, and drove the seven miles from this to the lower end of the glen. The whole of these seven miles are beautiful, both in their marine prospects, and their fringing of rock and wood, down to the very shores. The girls walked up the glen, till they reached a queer manufactory (not going) of Barytes. I went on a good deal further, but was obliged to return for them. Maitland and Davidson went up the whole of Sannox and down Glenrosie,—a severe, but admirable walk. These two glens—which hold Goatfell in their arms—are of the same character; rough with marsh and rock, roaring with water, and gloriously hemmed in by black splintered peaks.

It has been a calm delicious bright day, and Davidson and I retire for the night, resolved to be once more on the top of Goatfell, if the weather pleaseth, to-morrow. We should have been there to-day, if the morning had told us that after eleven the summit was to be so clear as it has been. I again walked, between four and six, round this bay. The south side is, beyond dispute, the best. But my exploration was suddenly stopped by discovering that a letter which I had written, addressed, and sealed, on the 4th inst., to the Provost of Glasgow, announcing the Circuit, and requiring him to process within his own burgh, on Thursday first, was still in my pocket. I was too late for the post, and had just time to hasten home, and give the letter, crumpled as it was, to a person who was stepping on board the steamer, and was to be in Glasgow to-night. I *rather suspect* that I would have stormed if anybody else had done this.

Ardrossan, Tuesday Night, 13th September 1842.—To-day was another yesterday, so far as concerned the enjoyment of the seashore regions, but warm lazy clouds lay on the hill-tops. After lounging therefore on the beach till two, Davidson and I set off and walked to Lamlash; after viewing which, we embarked in the steamer,—went back to Brodick, but did not land, took in the rest of the party, and, bidding adieu to Arran, were here by seven.

Lamlash is quietly placed, and this is its only recommendation. No, it has also a more gravelly beach than Brodick, the only defect of which is, that a line of paltry swamp is interposed between the beach and the houses. In every other respect Lamlash is far inferior to its rival capital; particularly in want of wood, want of high hills, and want of scattered cottages. These last,—the humble, but clean, white cottages, that are tossed about, each occupied by a comfortable idler,—form the peculiar charm of Brodick.

Henry Cockburn, Lord Cockburn (1779-1854) *Circuit Journeys* (Edinburgh: David Douglas, 1888)

Brodick Fair

Ayr Observer, 1847

The intercourse (in summer daily) with the mainland has greatly worn off the peculiar traits of the Islanders; and every fair they appear less singular, more improved, and better appointed in their turnout than on the previous one. Their simple carts are being superseded by properly constructed vehicles. The rude harness of rope, hair, or rushes, is being replaced with the civilised article. The home-made dress is giving place to more stylish manufactured fabrics.

The refreshment tents were very numerous. Teetotalism also had its representations in coffee tents. Goods stalls were abundant. The crowd of wooden dishes, cogs, and platters exposed for sale, show the prudence of old habits; and that the cleanly earthenware is too costly and breakable to displace the wooden bowl.

There were crowds of gambling stands. Penny reels absorbed much spare cash. The hardy and red-faced mountain nymphs footed it rarely, with stylish partners from the great city of Glasgow.

In the evening the islanders held their athletic games. There were four steamers with full freights of pleasure seekers from Ayrshire and Glasgow—the most of whom, however, returned in the afternoon before the more boisterous sports commenced.

Ayr Observer 29 June 1847

A Week in Arran
J. Smith, 1847

A lovely autumnal Sabbath morning, 'Serene, in all its dewy beauty bright', after a day and night of almost incessant storm and rain, greeted our enraptured vision. Slowly the mists were wreathing off Goatfell's hoary top and the clustering peaks that range beside it, half revealing the wildly picturesque scenery of Glen Rose and Glen Cloy, down whose sides a hundred night-born torrents were gushing. The waters of Brodick lay sparkling in the rising light, as the gentle breeze stirred their bosom, while the little low whitewashed cottages of the village, partially catching the struggling sunbeams, appeared in beautiful lustrous contrast to the dark foliage of the fir and plane trees by which they are shrouded. A few boats lay moored in the harbour, whose tall masts gently nodded to the breeze, and a number of small craft were hauled up on the golden strand. The gulls floated undisturbed over the wave; no footstep alarmed the solitary heron, 'the fisher of the wilderness', at his watchful perch. Everything breathed that serene quiet so peculiar to the day of rest, unless it were that now and then you heard the echoing bleat of the sheep afar off, or the scream of the curlew from his watery rest, sounds that lend a charm to silence. By and by, however, unusual appearances of life and animation were exhibited on the roads leading to the village—unusual, for it was yet early,—and seldom the quiet of the Sabbath morn is broken upon in rural districts till the distant noise of kirk bell proclaims the hour of worship. Long trains of light carts and cars, loaded with men and women, from different parts of the island, lined the road leading to Brodick, and solitary herdsmen and pedestrians came straggling across the moors by bye-paths and sheep tracks, bent for the same destination. On inquiry, we learned it was the Free Kirk Sacrament Sabbath, and that the people were gathering to it. As the morning advanced the numbers gradually increased; fewer convey-ances appeared, but more foot passengers proceeded along the roads, walking in little groups, with slow measured pace; the father leading his family by the hand, and the mother carrying her Bible wrapped in its snowy covering. A short time previous to the hour at which we were informed the services commenced, we set out with a friend who acted as our cic-erone, having some acquaintance with the locality. On arrival at the place of worship we found two congregations, English and Gaelic, assembled. The former, and smallest, met in a saw-pit, and the other in a meadow about four hundred yards distant. After hearing an eloquent and impres-sive discourse from one of the Free Church ministers from Edinburgh, we strolled leisurely forward to where the Highlanders were met. It was, in-deed, a picturesque and interesting scene to witness this assemblage, ren-dered doubly so by the peculiarities of the locality in which they were. Behind rose the towering heath-clad mountains, shelving down almost to the very spot. On one side ran a little stream gurgling over its pebbly course; and on the other, a long dark plantation of firs bounded them, and in front stretched out the waters of the bay. It reminded one of the hill-side gatherings in olden times of the children of the Covenant. About, as near as may be guessed, two thousand people of all ages, from the grey sire, on whose furrowed brow time had sown his scars, to the prattling child—sat upon the green sward, listening to the fervid natural eloquence of the preacher, poured forth in the language of the heart. Indeed, as a language, judging from its effects, there are few more calculated to arouse the feelings, to strike the hidden chords of the heart, and awaken slum-bering sympathies, than the Gaelic. On the females in the present case was this most observable, some of whom, rolled in their dark cloaks, and their white head-gear gathered closely around their faces, rocked a slow accompaniment to the not unmusical intonation of the speaker. Others evinced their more excitable disposition by low moanings and sharp hys-teric screams. But, on the whole, setting aside all that might be deemed fanatical enthusiasm, there was far more devotion exhibited by the na-tives than was apparent among the more tutored and civilised lowland audience. As we turned to depart, a Psalm was given out, and in a minute more the plaintive coronach-like music was wafted along on the breeze. There was something so utterly inartificial and sweetly mournful in the tune, breaking out in long fitful strains from female voices, and anon, as the men joined, rolling in fuller volume, that we stood for a time rivetted to the spot—even yet it rings in our ears. There was one thing gratifying to observe—the total absence of all those means of desecrating the sacred institutions which once, and we fear in some rural districts still, disgrace the religious profession of the worshippers, affording a strong argument to the satirist for turning the holiest rite into ridicule.

*

Fishermen's Huts by James Ferguson, 1842

Our main object in going to the island—for we may as well make a clean breast of it—was piscatory. Many flattering accounts of wonderful takes had reached our ears afar off, and we had resolved to test the truth of flying rumours by personal investigation. A friend, zealous in the art, had promised to join us, and cross the island—the only streams and lochs of any importance lying on that side. The weather on the morning after his arrival, just as good luck would have it, proved what the brethren of the gentle art rejoice in. All night and that day the rain descended in torrents, without the slightest intermission or faintest prospect of a relapse. It was considered, after some consultation, out of the question to walk to the burns—the nearest of which was nine miles distant—but, resolved not to miss such a promising opportunity, we, with some difficulty, induced the proprietor of a car to drive us part of the way. We set out, cheered by the prospect held forth by our conductor, that 'she was a gran weather for feeshin'—a fact, from long experience we were sufficiently aware of. No one of your warmth-loving townsmen need ever face the Highlands in quest of sport, if he desire a dry back. One and all of its streams and lochs never fish to perfection except in rainy weather.... The only trouting waters, we have already observed, are situated on the west side of the island. Of these the three principal streams are Blackwater, Mauchry, and Iorsa. Our destination was first to Mauchry, being the nearest. The road thence from Brodick lies principally up hill, running alongside a long range of mountains. Beneath you, after gaining the ascent, stretches a deep glen, where the Mauchry rises. On the opposite side springs up another range of high precipitous hills. As we

45

drove through this defile we saw few of its beauties. A dense heavy drizzling mist had settled down. At times a blast of wind lifted it up like a curtain from the hill sides, revealing a mass of dark rock and heath; at others, you were privileged with a glimpse of some yawning gulf beneath you, down which a mountain torrent was careering madly. Everything was blank, dreary, and uncomfortable; even the rain seemed not content with wetting one, but soaked in to the very joints. Repeatedly was the inquiry put by our junior friend, who had never previously been so highly favoured, 'Do you think there is any chance of it clearing up?' 'Hoo, 'tweel, it whiles rains this way an aicht days, but maybe 'till clear too!' was the invariable comforting assurance of the driver. Occasionally the dim outline of a human figure flitted by us, like a spectre, on the road, muttering, 'A wet morning.' Coming down the hill we encountered an angler returning home, excessively woebegone in aspect. On hailing him, in passing, we were informed that he had lost his way in the moors, been out all night, and left a companion lying at the back of a dike nearly dead. By and by we met another figure crawling along, his nether garments hanging in tatters, looking, by all the world, the type of despair, who gave himself out as the individual who had lain down to die in the moor. On day light coming in, it seems he had thought better of it. A mouthful of anti-teetotal liquor revived him wonderfully, and he pursued his homeward route. There was not, to be sure, much encouragement in all this; but anglers have been proverbially, from Ryp Van Winkle downwards, a hopeful body, and not easily deterred by unpromising appearances. Our driver set us down within sight of the stream, about three miles from its foot, and wishing us a successful fishing and a continuance of fine weather, returned homewards. One invigorating pull at the grey-beard, which had suffered considerably on the way, our creels strapped firmly on, and we were under weigh. We waded along about half a mile through long wet heather, sometimes almost waist high, ere we reached the stream, which, running through a broken rugged channel, is at all times rapid, but now, swollen with heavy rains, roared and foamed along terrifically. As we gazed into its dark, surging, boiling pools and eddies, madly whirly and dashing among the rocks, we felt ourselves instinctively shrink backwards. It was vain to think of fishing that part. No line would for an instant lie on its surface, setting aside the danger of attempting it, which was great enough, as a single false step would to a certainty have hurled the fisher into eternity. We turned away and struck into a sheep track, leading along its side. Pursuing this track through moss and brake, for better than two miles, with the rain still heavily descending, we came upon a fine open tract of country, fronting Kilbrannan Sound. Here the turbulent stream, finding a more level channel, had settled down considerably. To our delight a strong breeze arose and the rain gradually subsided. On again approaching the water we perceived a party of anglers hard at work. Not a moment was lost. Up went the rods and we fell to, though, for our own part, we admit to having felt a little chagrined at the dark opaque colour of the stream, inspiring sundry doubts in our mind as to whether even a red palmer would take…. Having some hope, as the water was clearing, that the trout would rise we adopted two favourite flies—a brown palmer and dusky yellow body and wing, ribbed with black hackle and tinsel. These will succeed with sea trout under almost any circumstances, and if you are ignorant of the taking fly on any particular stream no better choice could be recommended. We found them answer in the present case. The trout rose freely, and ere gloaming we had a respectably filled creel. After a little hunting about, lodgings were procured in the clachan at the foot of the stream. At a blazing peat fire, suggestive of great comfort, we got dried, and our inward man invigorated with a cup of tea. Afterwards, over a glass of something hot, we compared notes, and speculated on next day's chances, till the snoring of one of the party, from a corner, reminded us of bed.

*

Iorsa was in glorious trim. We fished up to the source, a small loch…. During the day, when the sun was strong, some of our company had felt a little nervous from stumbling over snakes among the heather. They are exceeding plentiful in the island. We saw them basking in the sun on every sheep track almost. There are two kinds—yellow and black; the former is harmless, but the bite of the other is very painful. Another annoyance, however, sprung up at sunset equally bad, and from a very ridiculous source. The air literally swarmed with midges, or *houlacs*, as they are in Gaelic graphically designated. It was absolute torture to stand still a single moment; our hats and coats were white with them. We have indistinct visions still of seeing two of the party seated on huge boulders, scrubbing away at their faces and throats, as if for life and death, with countenances horribly contorted and ghastly with smoking too many cigars. No whisky rubbed on the visage, or tobacco smoked, would drive them off. On they came with vampire lust in scores and hundreds. It was vain to calculate how often we lighted a pipe of about an inch long, and raised a cloud in the vicinity of our eyes and nose, but it ended all in smoke. There is but one remedy for this, and we had overlooked it in leaving the regions of civilisation—a thin gauze veil. It affords a complete safeguard against the annoyance. We have often wondered, in some deep glen, when, at evening, pursuing our quiet sport under grievous affliction, why the code of barbarity of former times never numbered amid its many horrible inventions for torturing humanity, that of exposing victims bound naked to midges. There is something ridiculous in the idea, but we believe the suffering in such a case would be little inferior to flaying alive.

J. Smith, ed. *Domestic Scenes…in Different Shires of Scotland* (Glasgow: George Gallie, 1847)

47

A Tamer Scene

Anonymous, 1848

If Nature long in mountain majesty
And wild attire beheld, fatigue the eye,
And we would choose a tamer scene t'embrace,
Then come with me; together let us trace
The streamlet to its source that winds along
Through deep Glen Sherig, where the cuckoo's song
Is heard all day the yellow broom among.
Come, let us labour up, and out of breath,
And panting, let us tread the budding heath,
The treacherous marsh with patience winding round,
And slowly circling every rising ground;
Resting at times, then labouring up again,
And clambering on till we the summit gain:
Then with the sparkling stream, that bickers on
Through moss and moor, and over rock and stone,
Trotting away right cheerily and brisk,
'Mong meads and hillocks, where white lambkins frisk,
The pastoral valley let us wander through,
Till Shiskin's corn-fields open on our view.

Sweet is the pastoral vale, its verdant hills,
With herds and wandering flocks, its gurgling rills,
Like diamonds sparkling in the sunny beam,
While hurrying on to join the flowing stream.
There is a beauty, too, in which the mind
Delights at times, though different in kind,
In the plain field, and cultivated farm,
Albeit devoid of all romantic charm:
The well-thatch'd farm-house, with its stacks behind,
All tightly built, and shelter'd from the wind;
Its barns and carts, and in the field hard by,
Its ploughs, and instruments of husbandry;
The horse, patient of injury, that stands,
Waiting his collar and the boy's commands;
The feathery tribes, speckled and white, that crowd
Around the measured dole, all cackling loud;
The mastiff strong, sagacious and alert,
Accustom'd to his chain; the terrier pert,
That snuffs about to see if all is right,
Wagging his tail, and barking with delight.

The various fields, well shelter'd, and fenced round,
Regular yet rural; where art is found
With Nature all harmoniously to blend,
And each the other a new charm does lend.
The wurzel here, the carrot, or the swede,
Planted in drills; on which the oxen feed,
And woolly tribes, when winter fierce comes on,
With frost and snow, and storms that quench the sun.
Potatoes too, prolific, wholesome root!
More precious than the tropic's choicest fruit;
Seen in the field, beautiful as the vine,
More valuable far, when stored, than wine.
The numerous tribes culmiferous; the hay,
With clovers interspersed, all waving gay;
Barley, and oats, and graceful rye; the tall
Rich wheat, fit staff of life; and, last of all,
The papilionaceous race, that pendent lean
On the black-eyed, delicious-smelling bean.

*

There was a freshness in the air while yet
The sun was vertical; but when he set
With all his blushing glories in the west,
The breeze fell calm, and ocean sank to rest.
And now, as if some talismanic wand
Had conjured up the antipodes; the strand,
The shore, the boats, the rocks, the fields, the trees;
Birds, cattle, people, houses, villages,
And hills, and dales, and the embosom'd bay,
And all the landscape, fair inverted lay.

*

We skimm'd the wave; and wonders now were seen
We dreamt not of,—a landscape submarine,
As if in crystal shrined; umbrageous, vast,
And varied: where Imagination traced
Brushwood, and bosky dell, forest, and grove,
With lawns between, for Nereids meet to rove;
And Fancy, ever playful, could discern
Terraqueous verdure, grass, and moss, and fern,
And heath, and birch, and, overhanging these,
Oak, ash, and pine, and all the forest trees.
Oh, who can tell the wonders of the deep?
What gems and beauties there unheeded sleep!

*

But now, beyond the hill which intervened

Awhile to circumscribe our sight, and screen'd
The loadstar of the landscape from our view,
Goatfell appears in Evening's magic hue.
Sweet are the hills at matins' holy hour,
And fair at high noontide; but there's a power,
A depth, a latitude of loveliness
Wraps them at eve, no language may express;
An aerial beauty which the soul does feel,
But scarce to thought can shape, cannot reveal.
And such their aspect, such the spell they wove,
While, like the eye of Evening, Hesperus o'er
Their summit shone, and on the isle did burn
The beacon-light, warning us to return.

Anonymous *The Isle of Arran: A Poem*. Cantos I and II (Edinburgh: Fraser & Co., 1848)

Glen Sannox

Alexander Smith, 1848

Next morning I rose early and looked forth:
The quiet sky was veiled with dewy haze;
Beneath it slept the dull and beamless sea;
The flowers hung dim and sodden in the dew;
Strange birds fed in the walks, and one unseen
Sang from the apple-tree. I dressed in haste;
And when the proud sun fired the dripping pines,
I wandered forth, and drank with thirsty eyes
The coolness of the sun-illumined brooks
In which the quick trout played. The speckless light,
The beauty of the morning, drew me on
Into a gloomy glen. The heavy mists
Crept up the mountain-sides; I heard the streams;
The place was saddened with the bleat of sheep.
"Tis surely in such lonely scenes as these,
Mythologies are bred. The rolling storms—
The mountains standing black in mist and rain,
With long white lines of torrents down their sides
The ominous thunder creeping up the sky—
The homeless voices at the dead of night

Wandering among the glens—the ghost-like clouds
Stealing beneath the moon—are but as stuff
Whence the awe-stricken herdsman could create
Gods for his worship.' Then, as from a cup,
Morn spilt warm sunshine down the mountain-side.
Cuckoo! cuckoo! woke somewhere in the light;
I started at the sound, and cried, 'O Voice!
I've heard you often in the poet's page—
Now, in your stony wilds—and I have read
Of white arms clinging round a sentenced neck
Upon a morn of death; of bitter wrong
Freezing sweet love to hate; of fond ambition
Which plaits and wears a wretched crown of straw,
And dreams itself a king; of inward shame,
To which a lingering and long-drawn death
Were bed of roses, incense, and a smile.
With anxious heart I hear my distant hours
Gather like far-off thunder. Canst thou tell
What things await me on my road of life
As did your floating voice?' Behold the sea!
Far flash its glittering leagues, and 'neath the sun
There gleams from coast to coast a narrow line
Of blinding and intolerable light.
I lay beneath a glimmering sycamore
Drowsy with murmuring bees.—As o'er my limbs
There palpitated countless lights and shades,
I heard the quiet music of the waves,
And saw the great hills standing dim in heat.

At height of noon a gloomy fleece of rain
Was hanging o'er the zenith. On it crept,
Drinking the sunlight from a hundred glens;
Blackening hill by hill; smiting the sea's
Bright face to deadly pallor; till at last
It drowned the world from verge to verge in gloom.
A sky-wide blinding glare—the thunder burst—
Again heaven opened in a gape of flame;
Heavy as lead came down the loosened rain—
I heard it hissing in the smoking sea;
It slackened soon, the sun blazed through, and then
The fragment of a rainbow in the gloom
Burned on the rainy sea—a full-sail'd ship
Apparent stood within the glorious light
From hull to highest spar. The tempest trailed

His shadowy length across the distant hills:
The birds from hiding-places came and sang,
And ocean laughed for miles beneath the sun.

Alexander Smith (1829-1867) from 'A Boy's Poem', *City Poems* (Cambridge: Macmillan, 1857)

On Seeing the Tower of Pladda Lit for the First Time

John Fergusson, 1849

Thou little orb that shin'st so bright,
And giv'st thy beauty to the night,
    When light reclines with day,
Propitious, happy be thy reign,
And long thy splendid blaze maintain,
    To shed the cheerful ray.

Unmov'd, unaw'd, thou'lt stand secure,
The stranger's friend, the beacon sure,
    To show surrounding fate;
Nor shall base art seduce thy smile,
Nor from thy duty e'er thee wile,
    To favour love or hate.

The moon and stars may hide their head,
And each celestial light seem fled,
    Or hid among the clouds;
But nought shall mar thy lovely light,
Nor stop those rays that shine so bright,
    From falling on the strouds.

When tempests roar and seas run high,
And topsails all to ribbons fly,
    Before the squalls of night,
The stranger fears the deep around,
Till from the watch the joyful sound,
    'Behold! there's Pladda light!'

But Cook, Macneil, how happy you,
When o'er the deep this comes to view,
    In calm or yet in storm!
The joys of youth, long laid at rest,
Shall then rekindle in your breast,
    When Arran shows its form.

Beloved land! the boast of isles,
Where virtue reigns and freedom smiles
    'Mong men long reckon'd brave,
Thy fame is laid in deeds of yore,
When Bruce his standard nobly bore
    For freedom or a grave.

Thy braes, thy glens, thy rippling rills,
Thy tow'ring rocks and lofty hills,
    Must ever, ever please,
Till nature all her charms resign,
Or sordid cares the mind confine,
    And these in triumph tease.

O, Cook, blest aid to human woe!
The helpless' friend, the coward's foe,
    To noble deeds e'er bent,
Ev'n sons unborn shall hail thy name,
And add their tribute to thy fame,
    For mercy to the *Kent*.

Macneil, as kind, as brave, sincere,
To friendship true, to mem'ry dear,
    Unknown alike to fame,
Thou ev'n, with Cook, would'st nobly vie
To save the wretched, hear their cry,
    And gain a deathless name.

Shine on, sweet light! to cheer the deep,
When tempests rage, when tempests sleep,
    And guide the pathless way;
But may thy flame more brightly burn,
When Arran's wand'ring sons return,
    And hail thy cheerful sway.

John Fergusson *Poems: consisting of a series of interesting subjects; scenes and traditions in Arran; elegies, and other detached pieces* (Ayr, Irvine and Glasgow, 1849)

Picnic at King's Cove

Thomas Alexander, 1853

It was a beautiful morning in the last days of autumn, when three cars of ladies and gentlemen issued from R— Villa, *en route* for 'King's Cove', upon an excursion of pleasure.... On through Lamlash, thence to Glen Scorrodale they drove. It was a delightful drive from Lamlash to Glen Scorrodale. On went the happy party up through between the towering mountains, which rose like walls tapering away from their feet, upon whose sides grazed little clusters of sheep, in all their mountain freedom, pictures of rural and peaceful affection. Issuing from the glen on the opposite side of the island they passed through Lagg, a lovely little place, nestled in the valley, a little removed from the sea shore. They afterwards passed through Shisken into Blackwaterfoot, where the little party dismounted from the cars, and, having got them put up at its little inn, they proceeded on foot over a high terrace of rocks to the Cove; the shore being too perilous and difficult to walk, especially for the fair travellers.

It was a lovely sight that the little party, descending from the rocky height, were enabled to behold. From a height of more than five hundred feet towards the Cove, from the sea rose the rocks on which they stood; and as they looked from the terrible precipice below them into the sea, which dashed its waters with a flowing tide against the mighty stones and boulders, which were scattered in ruinous profusion along the margin of the sea upon the shore, it brought a feeling of deepest sublimity to their souls. The wild birds, alarmed by their approach, flew, frightened, out, and soared above them in alarming screams. As the party reached the bottom and looked up overhead, the sight was terribly imposing, and magnificently sublime. The appearance of the day rendered it more so, and the fair travellers could not look but with a shuddering dread upon the awful majesty of the huge rocks above them. Walking along the shore they soon reached the Cove. The sun, hitherto bright and dazzling, had become clouded in sultry gloom, and the wind blowing strongly shoreward, dashed the angry waves among the giant blocks of rock that strewed the pathway, and compounded a scene striking and namelessly sublime.

Entering the Cove they prepared their pic-nic, and fared sumptuously on the refreshments which they had brought with them. Right wilfully did they attack the victuals, and amid puns, and jokes, and edifying sentiments, the bread, and fish, and boiled ham, disappeared as if by magic.

After satisfying their palates, they had a dance in right earnest upon the floor of the renowned cave, and games and other sports followed in course. Thence dividing into pairs they issued from the cave, some walking along the shore to listen to the music of the waters, and talk of love, as a matter of course; some in search of the fern 'osmundis regalis', while others sat them down upon some grassy plot 'to gaze across the sea', where Ireland could be dimly discerned through the sultry haze of that autumnal day.

Thomas Alexander *Charles Gordon; or, The Mask of Friendship. A Tale of Real Life* (Glasgow, 1865)

Sweet Arran's Isle

Anonymous, 1859

Air—I've Journeyed over many Lands

I have been in many distant lands,
    And many friends I've met,
But the hour I left sweet Arran's Isle,
    I never can forget.
Sweet are the thoughts when true love burns,
    Within a faithful breast,
But sweeter far when true love burns,
    And grateful love expressed.

Chorus—Oh Arran's hills and Arran's dales,
        And Arran's hills for me,
        Oh, take me back to Arran's hills,
        Arran's Isle for me.

I've climbed Ben Lomond's bonny hills,
    I've climbed them o'er and o'er,
But I'll come back to Arran's Isle,
    To that sweet rocky shore.
For in that isle there lives but one,
    One that I dearly love,
But his heart is to another
    More constant than the dove.

Chorus—Oh Arran's hills and Arran's dales,
        And Arran's hills for me,
        Oh, take me back to Arran's hills,
        Oh Arran's Isle for me.

But now I'll leave that lonely isle,
    And the many friends I've met,

For they have been so kind to me,
　　How can I e'er forget.
Oh, no, I'll ne'er forget that day,
　　I came to Arran's shore,
'Twas then I saw my first sweet love,
　　I ne'er shall see him more.

Chorus—Oh Arran's hills and Arran's dales,
　　　　Oh Arran's hills for me,
　　　　Oh Arran's hills and Arran's dales,
　　　　Sweet Arran's Isle for me.

Anonymous. Printed by the Poet's Box, 6 St Andrew's Lane, Glasgow 20 August 1859

A Delightful Visit to Lamlash

Lewis Carroll, 1871

Sept: 15. (F). An eventful day, to be marked 'with a white stone'. I had written to Sir Noel Paton mentioning an intention of coming to Arran, and had given him time to answer in case he liked to offer a bed. Not hearing, I thought I had better try a call, and went to Glasgow last night, sleeping at the 'Queen's'. This morning I got up at 6.30 and reached Lamlash about 11, left my bag at the little inn, and walked up to Glenkill House. My reception was as kind as it could be: I just came in for Mr and Mrs Craik, who had intended staying longer, but were hurrying home because Mrs Craik had sprained her ankle badly. They had arranged a sail for the afternoon, that the Craiks might see a 'long sea line' laid and taken up, and it ended in *my* being the fortunate spectator, and giving up my first plan, the returning by the 3 p.m. boat. The sail gave me a further opportunity of taming the children, who are rather shy at first, but the most unique 'children of nature' I ever saw, and perfectly charming. I was good friends with all, when I left at night, chiefly however with the eldest girl, Mona. The sail was most agreeable, and the drawing up of the sea-line (about 700 yards of cord, with 1,000 hooks) quite a new and interesting ''sperience', though a very small percentage (not five) of the hooks had any fish on them. Some of us landed on Holy Island, and Sir Noel and I visited the Hermit's Cave there. In the evening a friend of theirs came in, a Mrs Patterson with three children—they were very pleasant also. The whole visit was delightful, and an event to be long remembered. Slept at Lamlash Inn.

Holy Island by W. Noel Johnson, 1894

*

Sept: 19. (Tu). Off by the early train for Arran. Put up at the Broderick Hotel, and drove over to Glen Sannox, but we had wretched weather—nothing but mist and rain.
Sept: 20. (W). Went by boat to Lamlash and spent two or three very pleasant hours with the Patons. Back to Glasgow.

Lewis Carroll (Charles Dodgson 1832-1898) *Diaries* (1871)

Glen Sannox Adventure
William Mitchell, 1874

Of all our excursions, that from Glen Rosie into Glen Sannox is the one most worthy of being recorded. I was quite ignorant of the difficulty and even danger of this undertaking. I had fancied a pleasant ramble for several miles amid the wild scenery of the Arran hills, and then a scramble up some rocky defile, leading from the one glen into the other, of tolerably easy accomplishment. How different was all this from the reality.

It was well on towards mid-day when we set out, three of a party,—my wife, her sister, and myself,—I with a bag of provender strapped over my shoulder, and a staff, my two lady friends with nothing save their light umbrellas, and all of us in easy walking costume. The weather was delightful, and not too warm. We entered Glen Rosie by the fir plantation which slopes down into Glen Shant; here for some distance we were sheltered from the sun. The aroma of the firs was most agreeable. We emerged at a point well up on the hill-side, but at once descended and followed the course of the Rosie Burn, which threads its way right through the centre of the glen. At first the ground is soft and velvety, but as we proceed it becomes more rugged; patches of heather alternated with mossy grass, and large tracts of the common fern clothe the bottom of the glen. A footpath has been pretty well worn for some distance, but becomes gradually more and more rough and imperceptible. At its entrance the glen runs from east to west, but quickly curves round, and its main direction is north and south. At this curve the appearance and character of the glen materially alters. Whatever traces of life and cultivation may have been found at the outset, they are now completely lost. We saw neither the face of man nor beast, not even a shepherd's hut, from this point to our journey's end. It is here the Garbh Allt comes tumbling precipitously down into the Rosie Burn from the Ben Nuis range on the left. We stand on the plank bridge thrown across it, and admire the tumultuous torrent, which, in spite of huge rocks, forces a passage, laughing and mocking at every restraint.

Every human interest seems now shut out, and we are brought face to face with nature. We seem surrounded by an amphitheatre of hills. To the right the ranges of Goatfell slope down into the glen, and are dotted over with a shower of large stones, about the size of cannon balls. To the left the slopes of Ben Tarsuinn are studded with boulders of immense size, which seem to have been suddenly arrested, just in the act of rolling into the valley. Many have rolled down, and there are some singular specimens of huge natural monoliths standing like sentinels in the very path of the traveller. Before us are seen the sharp outlines of Keer Vör and the ridges which connect these several mountain chains together, and we begin to wonder where the pass can be which will admit us from Rosie into Sannox.

The burn, whose windings we now follow, is a source of constant pleasure, both from its gentle murmur, so refreshing to the pedestrian, and from the new and varied aspects in which it so continually presents itself. Deep pools, gently flowing currents, cascades, and waterfalls follow one another in quick succession. Sometimes it flows by the side of flat gravelly banks, and anon it has to force its way through deep crevices and rocky fissures. Now naked and bare, and again ornamented with all the gaiety and beauty of a bride, when shrubs and ferns of the freshest green, and occasional wildflowers, hang over and adorn its sparkling countenance. The water was so bright and clear, that one could trace the outline of all the nooks and crannies in the rocks over which it ran, or in the pools where it rested; the very pebbles lying at the bottom might have been counted. The strange manner in which the stream had worn and shaped the rocky bottom often gave rise to fantastic suggestions. In the centre of one large beautifully clear pool lay a block of stone bearing the shape of a gigantic salmon. Here, said we, will lie the memorial of some mighty king of fishes, to whom the trout of Glen Rosie have raised this monument. Cheerfully and happily we trudged along until our approach to the head of the glen apprised us that it was time to hold a council of war as to our further progress.

Keer Vör here bars the way, and sends ridges down, joining the Goatfell range on the one side, and the Ben Nuis on the other; and with a pretty steep ascent, the bottom of the glen slopes up to the base of these rocky barriers. We were in doubt whether the ramparts were to be scaled by the coll or ridge on the right or on the left of Keer Vör. My vote would have been given for that on the right; but one of my fair friends had been in the glen before, and seen *somebody* point to a fissure on the left as the usual route; so I yielded to this strongly expressed opinion. In passing, I may say I am now convinced we did wrong, and I much doubt if the route we now chose for ourselves had ever been trodden by human foot before.

The council having been thus concluded, and fighting resolved upon, we sat down by the burn to refresh and brace ourselves for the task. I did not allow my wallet to be emptied, although this would have made my walking easier, but, like a prudent general, I husbanded my resources, not knowing what drain there might yet be upon them.

We found the ascent towards the defile, whither we now bent our steps, very arduous and rugged: it was enough of itself to try our mettle, before even reaching the formidable-looking gully where we hoped to find an outlet. When we got close to this fissure, my survey of it was anything but reassuring. It seemed a crack in the mountain side caused by some convulsion of nature, and was filled with immense blocks of stone, piled upon and jammed into one another—a perfect Ossa upon Pelion, with summit in the skies. The angle, also, was so great that if the first climber dislodged any loose stones or debris they could not fail to roll down, to the imminent danger of those following. Nor was it possible at any part of it to see more than a very short distance a-head, or to judge of its probable length or issue. Altogether it had a very ugly look. Two considerations, however, urged us on. On looking back we could see the long weary way we had already traversed; while this cleft in the rock might be a short and sharp exit, and entrance into a new, interesting, and to us entirely unexplored region. Again, if there was one thing more than another my fair friends dreaded, it was defeat. The thought of returning with hanging heads and trailing pikes seemed to them far more dreadful than any difficulties that shewed themselves.

In Indian file, I of course the leader, we made the start. The blocks of stone had either to be circumvented or scrambled over, according to their size. Hands and arms as well as feet were in constant play. Sometimes we had to drag one another up where the rocks were more than unusually high, or to steady one another as we turned some sharp precipitous corner. I did little to help the ladies, because, first, I could not well help both; and secondly, I found a little vocal encouragement, coupled with their own exertions and presence of mind, more efficacious than had I taught them to depend on my aid. Many a time, in fact, when I, far a-head and toiling on in haste and in anxiety, felt both sick and faint, the sound of their cheery voices below refreshed and reinvigorated me. Of course, I often halted and hailed them, and affected a light-heartedness I was far from feeling. Once or twice, but especially on one occasion, I had found my scrambling ascent so difficult that I did not see how they could possibly surmount it, and I shouted that we should have to halt and return. They replied, that to return was more impossible than to proceed, so we scrambled on. I lay down, overcome with giddiness and faintness, at the back of a large rock, while they pressed on to join me. My eagerness to get on overtaxed my strength; but after a few minutes' rest, and seeking help where it is always to be found, I started again. I was at last encouraged by a glimpse of what I took for a cairn of stones not far above me. There, thought I, is the goal, the beacon for the weary climber; so I whistled long and loud to my toiling companions, and shouted as if I had already reached it. A few more struggles and I gained the summit. My cairn, however, was only a large natural boulder, with no particular signification; and, although upon the top, I had not the faintest idea of where I was.

Having recovered breath, I at once retraced my steps to help and cheer on my companions, who, by shorter stages, had kept tolerably close upon my track. As we emerged from the gully we threw ourselves, thankful and panting, upon the stone-covered grassy slope, which to us was a perfect couch of repose after our exhausting efforts. Before many minutes I felt the necessity of surveying and exploring our position. I was utterly amazed and almost stupified at the altitude we had attained, the singular view on every side, and my utter ignorance of our whereabouts. I need not record the foolish mistakes I made in this hasty survey, but correct myself from inquiry and observation subsequently made.

To our right stood the crest of Keer Vör, whose riven side we had been so laboriously climbing. It had a curious, rugged, overhanging appearance, and seemed constructed of flat layers of rock laid one upon another, varying in size and shape, and always decreasing towards the top. Passing from this most conspicuous object, I can scarcely pretend to give even a faint outline of the singularly superb scene by which we were surrounded. We were in the very heart of all the mountain groups and ranges of the island. The glens of Rosie, Sannox, and Iorsa all radiated from this point, and with a slight change of position we had them full in view. Two fresh water lochs lay high up among the hills towards the west and north, and the sea was visible on every side.

My anxiety, however, as to our future progress was too great to admit of unmixed feelings of delight, and I proceeded with but little delay to explore a passage, if possible, into Sannox. The search for the north-west passage was never more ardently pursued by Arctic explorer. My first survey led me to the ridge which encircled the upper part of the glen, and was most discouraging. Sheer rocky precipices formed its boundary apparently on every side, and guarded against all intrusion. I was almost despairing. No sense of the grandeur of the scene could take possession of me. I felt that the safety of others had been imperiled by my foolishness, and I was constantly blaming my rashness. I wandered on, trying to find some fissure or less precipitous slope down which we might creep, and at length a sort of sheep track met my eye. This led me to the left shoulder of the glen, where several white gravelly courses, like the dry bed of a mountain torrent, sloped down not absolutely in a perpendicular direction. Here I paused and signalled for my companions, who were slowly following me, that I might hold another council. One of them at once took heart and pronounced the breach practicable; the other thought it out of the question. As I had the casting vote, I put on as jaunty an air as possible, and at once proceeded to shew how, by spreading ourselves out as much as possible in a slanting or reclining posture, striking fingers and heels well into the stones, which were not large, and holding well together, we might safely get to the bottom. On making the attempt we found it rather irksome and trying, but not dangerous, and came soon to a less steep descent, where the water course ended amidst a bottom of grass and brechans, thickly interspersed with large stones. Here we threaded our way into what I fondly hoped to find the bottom of the glen. My next observation, however, again startled me. I found we had only got into the gallery, as it were, from the roof, and the area had still to be reached. Right in front there still stretched a new sunken barrier, and as we toiled along to reach it, we could form no opinion as to whether it might not effactually bar our way.

Here, thought I, is a nice trap into which I have brought my party. Failing this descent, nothing seemed possible for us but a *bivouac* for the night in our present quarters. Even had it been possible to reascend the ladder, the approach of night and our weary limbs would have precluded such an effort. It was already getting toward evening; grave and strange fancies filled my mind. What a sleeping apartment! Shall Goatfell then stand sentinel to-night, and guard these frail wanderers from the wild spirits of the glen? Shall Sannox draw his gloomy curtain round their heathery bed, and cause the mountain torrent to warble his sweetest lullaby while they slumber? It may be so, but even then, what cause for regret and fear? Are we not children of the land where the mist and the heather, and the mountain and the flood have their home? Have not our forefathers made dear to us these heaths and glens, and rocks, and caves? Yes, if need be, we shall rest here, and make Glen Sannox echo with our songs of praise.

Alone I hurried on. On reaching the ledge the burn leaped right over the face of the rock into the glen below. To the left of it the descent was precipitous and impracticable. Towards the right there was a broken piece of ground where some large stones held a precarious footing on a scrubby soil, and here I resolved we should attempt to scramble down. So, aiding one another, and hanging on to patches of scrub or heather, and getting occasionally steadied at the back of some large stone, we at long-length found ourselves at the base of the upper end of this most imposing glen. A long journey was still before us, but our dangers were ended, and with light hearts we sat down on a ledge of rock where the sparkling burn played around us. We rested, and also disposed of what my foresight had still retained in the wallet; nor did we fail to return thanks to that Heavenly Father who is ever the kind Protector of all who put their trust in Him.

It was now possible for me to allow my pent up feelings to overflow in fervent admiration of this wild picture, all of Nature's own. The last declining rays of the sun were reddening the tops of some of the highest cliffs, contrasting strangely with the gloom now gathering around us. A sense of solemn awe crept over me, as I gazed at these tremendous crags and precipices, bounding both sides of the glen. On high inaccessible rocks, the forms of two gigantic figures stood forth; and many a cave high up among the cliffs was quite as worthy of Fingal as those devoted to him in Skye. I was oppressed by a sense of my own littleness and feebleness. It seemed to me that a felt relation to God the Creator alone could overcome the feeling of utter weakness and helplessness which man must feel in the grasp of such stupendous forces....

On the walk through Glen Sannox I must not dwell. It was probably five or six miles in length. The knee-deep heather and the occasional boggy ground, with no footpath to guide us, made it arduous enough. The burn here, as in Glen Rosie, was both guide and friend. Now it rushed through deep chasms, and again it spread out like a fan and flowed gently over a large flat surface of rock, perhaps fifty or sixty feet square; here it fell sparkling from above, and there it wandered along in strange grooves of every imaginable shape, which it had cut for itself in its course.

We pushed on, however, without lingering much to admire, and ere the shade of night had quite enveloped us, we reached an old mill, which stands near the entrance of the glen. We found the bridges over the burns mostly broken down, which gave us a great deal of extra scrambling, but at length we came to the old churchyard, close to the shore, and, late and wearied as we were, we turned aside to look on the memento of those who had once formed a larger and more numerous population than now exists. We had not as yet been greeted by face of man or beast.

Having gained the main road, I warmly congratulated my fair friends on the energy and spirit which had carried them so well through. It was nearly ten o'clock, and we were still seven or eight miles from home; but at Corrie, which we soon reached, I got a conveyance; and seldom has jaunting car seemed so like a bed of down. The moon shed a soft luxuriant radiance on wood, and sea, and shore; and Nature, in one of her most gentle aspects, soothed our excited feelings. We reached home about eleven o'clock, tired but not exhausted, and were gladdened by the 'cup that cheers'. The clear invigorating air of the island has much to do with carrying one through a heavy day's work; and lengthened experience has taught me that stimulants, unless in some sudden emergency, are better avoided. Soon we pressed our grateful pillows, 'fought all our battles o'er again, and thrice we slew the slain'.

William Mitchell *A Fortnight in Arran* (Glasgow: Bell and Bain, 1874)

Goatfell
William Thomson, 1876

Here, from the peak of this canescent pile,
    A glorious panorama meets our gaze;
    The distant mountain-peaks, cradled in haze,
The streams, the valleys of this happy isle;
Bright in the summer dayshine, we can see
    The lucent bays, the hills in robes of heath,
    And the long-waving, singing surge, beneath
The fleecy clouds' trajecting tracery.
Yonder a castellated mansion lies,
    Shrined in the bosom of the verdant hills,
    'Mong woods alive with scented calcycles.
O happy isle! with hungry, longing eyes,
    I gaze upon you! Ere another day
    I'll tread yon smoky city far away.

William Thomson from 'Arran Sonnets' (1876) *Leddy May and Other Poems* (Glasgow, 1883)

The Picture Cave
William Lytteil, 1877

The Picture Cave has been sadly neglected by the describers of Arran, and I cannot refer to a single work in which it is mentioned. Consequently, when I managed to wrap myself through the strait and narrow aperture, which alone gives entrance to the inner crypt of this remarkable grotto, I felt as if something of the nature of a discovery had been made. Not a streak of light from the sun ever enters the cave, and the darkness within is as thick as the silence is profound. Sweet enough, however, is the atmosphere of the cavern, and by the help of a rush-light I explored it fully. Cones of stalactite, like icicles of spar, depend from the vault overhead, but not so numerously as in some caves. Its walls of red sandstone close solidly round it on every side, leaving only a narrow orifice at the bottom of a shaft by which admission can be gained; and even this cannot be effected without difficulty and a solemn feeling of imminent peril. For the entrance is formed by masses of rock, which have slipped down from above, and got jammed in the crevice below; but one can scarcely satisfy himself that a single piece of rock shall not be disturbed by a touch, as the adventurer scrambles through the aperture, and, coming down upon him like a portcullis, fix him as in a trap for ever. Nevertheless I went in, but only after carefully testing the solidity of the jaws and mouth-piece of the cavern. Scrambling up the narrow shaft, light in hand, my first feeling as I glanced into the dark recesses of the cavern—made even more pitchy black by the flicker of rush-light which filled the middle space—was one of indescribable awe. 'Here at last,' said I, 'is a cell for a hermit'; and I searched the walls of the crypt for crosses or sculpture of any kind, but found none. 'How then,' it may be asked, 'do you call it the Picture Cave?' Simply because the grand outer gallery or corridor of the cave is carved all over with men-of-war in full sail, others with sails furled and yards squared, while here and there, among the great three-deckers of the days of Cook and Nelson, cutters and brigs are cruising about in all the glory of canvas and bunting. Pretty mosses and tiny seedlings of the Hart's Tongue Fern, besides lichens and golden chrysosplene, adorn the massive walls of this romantic gallery; while all along over the eaves, as it were, of this charming Arcade, hang a great profusion of Holly fern (*Lastrea recurva*), purple-cymed grasses, St John's Wort, and other flowers. (All these were seen by me when I visited the Cave during my Christmas holidays of 1873. The beauty of the winter foliage of the evergreen Holly-Fern was such as one could never become weary of admiring, and today the fragrance of some fronds of it which I gathered at the time, is as purely sweet and refreshing as it ever was.) Could the *eident* carvers of these quaintly chiselled men-of-war return to the cave, they would see what a graceful drapery the hand of Nature has hung around their pictures; but since the dates incised upon the stone beside the ships, and the initials of the carvers, range from 1779 to 1791, there is not much chance of any of them being ever able to do so. Little doubt can be entertained that these figures and other carvings were executed by the miners who long ago quarried the cliff which is about two hundred and fifty yards to the north-west of the cave, and that while dwelling on this lonely shore they thus endeavoured to while away many of their leisure hours. (The length of the corridor or gallery which runs up to the cave's mouth, is about fourteen yards, and the width is about eight or nine feet.)

Ere I quitted the cave, and, as I may say, the heart of the mountain, I estimated the dimensions of the cavern at forty feet by forty, while the height of the vault appeared to be about twenty feet. I observed a dark passage running away into the hill from the inmost side of the cave, but it was much too strait to admit of further exploration.... A descendant of the former tenants of Kwee calls the Picture Cave by the simple Gaelic appellation of An-Uamh [an-oov], or The Cave. In front of it there is a small creek or port on the shore, beside a dyke of large stones, and a 'keppagh' or small tilled plot. From this creek to the famous stone called the Cock of Arran, the distance is about five or six hundred yards.

William Lytteil *Landmarks of Scottish Life and Language* (Edinburgh: J. Moodie Miller, 1877)

Art Rambles
John T. Reid, 1878

The Boat-house became my roosting-place while under the shadow of the mighty mountain of the wind, 'Goat Fell'. The lady of the house loved to be called by her Christian name, Martha, and she was not without traits in her character we are prone to associate with the name. She was careful and troubled about many things. In the summer season her troubles were born of her prosperity. Like the woman famed in the bairns' rhyme, 'who lived in a shoe, and had so many children she did not know what to do', Martha in her Boat-house kept so many lodgers—the cooking of meals, making of beds, and washing of linen for such a host made her often remark, 'I have so much wark, I dinna know what to do first'; and then she had a husband to work for. 'There's poor Archie, he canna dae a han's turn for himsel', and

The Boat-house, Brodick by J.T. Reid, 1878

I've to earn every bite o' bread he eats.' Yet Martha was a woman of courage, and she succeeded nobly in satisfying her hungry lodgers with wholesome fare, and spreading for them sheets a prince might fold around him; and though the body was often weak, the spirit was lively, and soon found a way whereby to mount with ease over any difficulty that might arise in the government of her household or the entertainment of her hospices.

*

From the sketch my reader will discover why this sea-cot was called the Boat-house: an upturned boat forms the roof, and under this roof is the but and the ben, the kitchen and the parlour, each boasting its own snug box-bed. The kitchen had one small window, the parlour two, one looking out over Brodick Bay, the other inland; joined to this main building were various outhouses, each having a door, a window, a box-bed, a small deal table, a candlestick, and a wash-basin of its own: these were let for the most part to single gentlemen, though now and again she had also lady lodgers. The surroundings were full of interest: in the foreground we had Martha's pig-store, where she kept a varied assortment of china and earthenware; it also was roofed by the remains of an old pleasure boat; Martha's cabbage garden and potato plot, and Martha's hen-house, where the roosters were alike honoured by having a boat-house of their own. A bank of sand separated between the sea and an inner expanse of shore, in which the bed of Rossie Burn was pillowed among undulating slopes clad with a profusion of sea-grasses; at full tide it seemed like a fresh-water lake, at ebb tide but a marshy waste, only the stream meandering along its time-worn groove.

*

The day set apart for the Lamlash trip was rather an unfortunate one, and brought vividly to mind the misfortunes that befell my respected drawing-master, who came to paint the Arran hills, but was day after day, through stress of weather, confined to the subject of the picture that figured on the walls of the Royal Scottish Academy in the following February, entitled, 'My Lodgings in Arran', for it rained constantly and heavily. I chose the road nearest the coast, and had many refreshing bits of dripping leafage and cliff and rural cottage retreat by the way; and after the hill was rounded, I got a very shadowy view of Lamlash Bay and Holy Isle. The latter did not suffer much from being so completely swathed in the cloudy spell; but the rather loomed great in size, and gave imagination licence to fill in details of majestic proportions. The potato-diggers were as wet as if they had been bathed in the bay with their clothes on. It was fair-day, and, despite the weather, the muddy road was thronged by eager folks from the rural districts, who were witnessing the competition for prizes, being adjudged to the horses that looked in the best condition, and who when running and trotting did not belie their looks; others were among the sheep-pens, and many fine specimens were ticketed with either a prize card or 'honourable mention'. The sole competitors in the swine department was a big lanky sow and her large family of young porkers. The mother was adjudged the first prize, the litter the second. The cattle had their stance a little distance away, and had been judged earlier in the day. The inns were redolent of whiskey and whiskey songs; many carts and gigs were waiting on the road-side, and in an hour or two Lamlash would be as quiet as is its wont, and the visitor of the season could enjoy his walk with his cousins, undisturbed by runaway animals and the gaze of the sons of the soil. I nearly omitted to mention that two young men passed through the streets, bearing in triumph between them, hanging on a rod, the body of an adder, about two feet long and one inch in circumference.

*

This morning I found one of the giant snails who pertinaciously laid siege to my cabin, with his head and horns buried in the roll of fresh butter in my larder; he was fully eight inches long; doubtless in the French market he would have found favour. I did not kill him, but gave him a place on the other side of the railing. These snails had a provoking way of paying nocturnal visits, and wandered between the wooden walls and the loosely fixed paper that decked the walls, making a noise that deceived me into the belief that they were just about to leave the wall for the bed-clothes, and that the next notice I might have of their movements might be a cold, clammy touch from one of them. Other friends I had, viz., a family of mice, that delighted themselves performing running feats and pedestrian excursions, that might have gained them fame in certain circles if they had been men instead of mice; and a sagacious hen in the broad daylight was ambitious to leave a new-laid egg in the corner of the hole in the wall I designated my cupboard.

John T. Reid *Art Rambles in the Highlands and Islands of Scotland* (London and New York: Routledge, 1878)

To Parties in Search of a Good Holiday
William McQueen, c.1880

Given; a young clerk on a small salary, with a week's holidays, and only thirty shillings or two pounds to spend—how can he make the most of his time and money?

Answer: Let him take the Campbeltown steamer and go to PIRN MILL.

For such an one there is no place on the coast to be compared to this part of Arran.

Very likely ere he lands he will be drenched with salt water as the small boat, which conveys him from the steamer to the exposed shore, leaps over the roaring breakers; and this first novel sensation will, in a few minutes, be followed by another as he is told to sit well towards the stern, while men on shore heave the boat through the shallow water by means of a primitive windlass in front of the ferry-house.

Once landed, carpet bag in hand, he will find himself in a region of sea and rock, and moorland and Gaelic; and his inquiry for a place to put up in will likely be answered by an assurance that lodgings are not to be had, and that he would have been better to land at Loch Ranza, seven miles further back, where there is an inn. Such an intimation need not daunt him, for he will likely, within an hour, find himself located in the room of a modest cottage, the window of which commands a view of the Sound of Kilbrannan, from Sanda to Ardlamont point; with a landlady bustling about to make him as comfortable as she can.

Now let us frankly confess, before going further, that Pirn Mill has its drawbacks. The flutter of silk and the bulge of a parasol are unknown; tooth-brushes and hair oil as yet are not; and a newspaper cannot be had for love or money. Then the butcher's van only passes twice a week, and loaf bread is occasionally unattainable. But these things only serve to render the change of life more complete and therefore more enjoyable. If loaves are not to be had, flour is, and the landlady will only be too glad to shew her skill in producing the most toothsome scones ever man tasted; and who cares for butcher meat every day if it can be alternated with a mess of eggs, so newly laid that they are not cold when transferred to the frying-pan? What poor clerk ever had such a dessert as he may obtain by going round to the back of the house and pulling without stint wild strawberries and raspberries, or brambles and hazel nuts? And if there be not a public house for miles, what does it matter, when there is a cow grazing on the sward before the door, and a burn runs past the side of the house, the water of which, even in the middle of summer, is as cold as ice and clear as crystal? Then where else on the coast could the Limited Holiday Man see the herring fleet taking up their stations in the evening almost within hailing distance of where he sits? And after darkness falls, what a weird sight it is to look seaward, and behold lights flashing up here and there for a moment, as the fishers dis-play their signals to warn neighbour fishermen from drifting down upon them. Let the strayer go down to the shore, and he will hear the, to him, unfamiliar sound of oars working in the rollocks, as the trawlers row past looming vaguely through the gloom within a hundred yards of the shore, and may perhaps see the *skinkle* of the fish as the net is hauled.

If our poor clerk be a swimmer, more clear and limpid water never invited bather to its bosom than laves the shore at Pirn Mill, the bottom being visible to any one standing on the beach for we would not like to say how far out.

The first day should be spent in the immediate neighbourhood. It is a region of abruptly rising waste, intersected by numerous small glens, the beds of which present a series of lovely little cataracts and pools, overhung by a wealth of hazel and fern and wild rose. If fly fishing be not practicable, the more exhilarating sport of guddling is; and what can be better than standing up to the knees in a burn, with coat off and shirt sleeves rolled up as high as they will go, trying to circumvent the *jinkings* of a spreckled trout among the stones at the bottom of the stream? Should you require a light to your briar-root, enter the first house you stumble upon (they are so perched in out-of-the-way places you always do stumble upon them), and you may find the proprietor weaving in a fashion as primitive as that of the Indians of Cashmere. Or on coming out, your attention may be arrested by a queer sound in the barn, and peeping in you may discover a man busy thrashing by the old process of the flail. Nor would we be surprised though you should be served, unasked, with a basin of rich milk before leaving by 'a lassie with eyes of Highland blue'.

On the second day Loch Ranza may be visited, and the seven miles' walk along the coast under butting cliffs perforated with gloomy caverns, the dark recesses of which are the theme of many a wild legend, is a thing to be remembered and talked about for a lifetime.

But it is at Caticol, two miles short of Loch Ranza, that the grandest view is to be obtained. A vast glen, many miles in extent, at the very entrance to which all verdure ceases, gradually opens on the right hand of the pedestrian. It is enclosed on three sides by stupendous mountains, bare of even heather from base to summit, but with basaltic patches here and there upon their shoulders, which glitter like burnished silver in the sun's rays. We know of no such scene of barren grandeur in Scotland. Hills of every shape, from the almost perfect cone to the most rugged and irregular, challenge our admiration and awe, and present such a prospect as can only be equalled by some parts of the coast line on the west side of South America. Make a man unconscious, carry him a mile up Caticol glen on a warm summer day, and get him to believe when he awakens that he has been asleep for three months: then ask him to guess from the surrounding scenery in what part of the world he is, and we wager he will fix on Arabia Petrea, or the Cordilleras, or any other place in the world before his native land.

By the third day his muscles will be in trim for a good climb, and he can choose his mountain for himself. Just let him go right up from the shore, fearless of being questioned for trespass (we don't believe the word has any synonym in Gaelic), and in a quarter of an hour he will find himself beyond even the region of footpaths, and in a land of mountain-gale and heather. Where else would he be at liberty to brush through the undergrowth, and rouse coveys of whirring grouse and partridge and black-cock, without let or hindrance? And surely the sheen of the brilliantly plumaged pheasant is not the less beautiful to him that he is not at liberty to spoil it with powder and shot; while his exercise and surroundings are at least equal to what many peers of England pay thousands of pounds to enjoy.

In a short time he will discover that various summits present themselves for his selection, each having special recommendations of its own; and there is a possibility that he may select one that has never been ascended by man before. If he manages to scale it, he may give it his own name if he please, and surely Ben Smith sounds as well as Ben Mhor. Then he *has* a view. From the Cloch to the North of Ireland, and from the Ayrshire coast across Kintyre to the Western Islands and the Atlantic, a hundred miles in length and fully seventy in breadth the prospect unfolds itself to his gaze. But what it is like we will not attempt to describe to him; he must go and see it or he can never know anything about it. Had the locality been Switzerland, and not a place within a 2s. sail of Glasgow, neither poet nor painter would have left it so long unnoticed.

Another day may be spent in visiting Auchancarr, a village seven miles to the south of Pirn Mill. It lies within 400 yards of the road which skirts the beach, and yet, so singular is its situation, one may pass along the road without being aware that there is a village in close proximity. In the neighbourhood of the place are three very large Druid stones, well worthy of careful inspection. And on the road to Auchancarr we pass Imachar, a little clachan perched upon a cliff, so steep and dark and frowning that it might have become famous in the hands of the author of the *Mysteries of Rudolpho*; and around the base of which the waves boil and hiss as in a cauldron.

But we need not go on to enumerate more particularly the various attractions of the district. Nowhere that we know of could a man with a limited purse secure that great desideratum, a complete isolation from everything calculated to recall his ordinary prosaic life; combined with everything calculated to awaken in his mind new emotions of delighted wonder and amazement. And in naming two pounds, we are sure we give the maximum sum at which all this might be purchased; while a careful man might quite well do it for thirty shillings, including fare both ways.

William McQueen [c.1880]

A Ramble Round Arran

(*A reminiscence of September, 1882*)

William Brown Smith, 1882

Our breakfast past, we leave fair Corriegills,
Friend Mayes and I, to scale the heath-clad hills:
Past dark Dun-dhu,—then up o'er green Dun-Fion
Where but a glance from Fingal's Fort takes in
Sufficient of a scene—surpassing fair—

To feast the imaginative mind,—yet there
We may not stay, so down the hill we go
Towards Lamlash that lieth far below;
Through fields where reapers cut, and bind the corn, in
Sheaves, saluting with a glad *'goot mornin''*,
As past we walk with joyous swinging stride
To reach the road, beside yon murm'ring tide,
Well sheltered, bounded by the Holy Isle,
And sloping mainland, bathed in sunlit smile.
Lamlash—we rest,—the steamers now arrive:
See! what a gay and bustling crowd contrive
To block, besiege, the quaint Post-Office door,
For news of friends upon the other shore,
Who toil, or spoil, in crowded towns together,
All glad, or sad, this grand September weather.
But 'tempus fugit', we must haste to dine;
Round by the Cordon bridge we soon recline
Beneath the rowans' berried leafy shade,
Beside the burn, meandering through the glade,
Where honey-suckle crowns the flowery lea,
Commingling with the ozone from the sea,
Whose sparkling wavelets gleam between the trees:
But we must go, and Whiting-bay with ease
We reach: the day keeps fine, *our heart's desire*;
We pass a man with pleasure boats for hire,
Who lazily leans his sturdy arms upon
Some poles, and with a Gaelic nasal tone,
The range of English words and grammar scorning,
Drawls out, 'To-day's—a fine—*pen-osh-les* morning.'
This last coined word, penoshles, takes by storm,
A gay discussion follows, as to form
And origin,—if Latin, Scotch, or Greek;
Most likely a linguistic *Hielan'* freak,
Which neatly put in some most solemn phrase,
Caused many a laugh throughout our holidays;
And now we're toiling up the winding road
Towards the Dippin Lodge, where many a load
Of game, etcetera, for *'her grace ta duke'*
Is *bagged*; and near this charming rock-bound nook
We rested on a ferny bank, when lo!
A flesher's van pulls up,—a face I know!
A friend of youth, Mat., greets with broad'ning smile,
Long missed—found here, amassing quite a pile
Of wealth; with temperance, care, and hard work earned;

Well wed—respected—afterwards I learned.
We round the turn and gain the last hill-top,
A moment here to gaze, with joy we stop,
On Pladda Isle and lighthouse far beneath,
And steamers' smoke, twining in many a wreath
Fantastic—borne by breath of coming gales,
Far, far away, past yonder ship, whose sails
Illumed at times by gleam of westering sun,
Reminds, that we life's changeful course must run.
We walk on past dark Bennan headland bold,
With lofty cave, where savages of old
Dwelt, making arrow-head and axe of stone,
To aid the chase, or carry warfare on:
Till later times, when worshipped here
Those who, for conscience' sake, lost much that's dear.
A waterfall leaps grandly near this cave;
Yon flagstaff marks the Warrior Poet's grave;
Here, Ossian, Fingal's son, old, blind and lone,
Wept, sleeps, where wind and wave, *coronachs*, moan.
On still we go, and soon, with glad surprise,
Lag's wood-hid classic hollow feasts our eyes,
Like alpine scene,—with white-washed cozy inn,
Its ancient cairn, and famous streams, within
Whose pools and eddies prime trout shyly swim,
Or leap to catch the flies that o'er them skim.
We cannot linger here, so seek friend Cook's,
At Slidd'ry School-house with its maps and books,
And sturdy youths, who learn right merrily,
Lore, gained in City University:
We enter in,—Oh! some mistake is here;
A school-house sure, ah me! it doth appear,
Tho' tired, we're wrong, and learn to our dismay,
That *his* is two miles further on our way:
We shortly ask a native, passing by,
The road and distance,—who, with pitying eye,
Says, 'You'll pe there py dark if you'll but push;
Keep straight along till you see a bush,—
Then turn a wee bit, to your left and right.'
'Thanks, thanks,'—ha! ha! we'll manage there to-night.
Stout hearts and limbs required, brave and strong,
For Arran miles are often *very* long;
Yes! many a bush we passed, turned right and left,
Altho' of precious daylight nigh bereft,
We gained our goal,—and after supper slept

Full soundly: yet the breakfast wasn't kept
Behind on our account. At nine we start,
With thankful hearts to Him whose loving care
O'ershadowing, crowns our walk with blessings rare.
We pass Kilpatrick-point and Feorline;
Above, *beneath*,—how fair th' Autumnal scene!
Blackwater-foot, next, fortressed Drumadoon,
King's Caves, where Bruce in exile lived, and soon
Tormore's stone circles with their Warrior's Urn:
Then rest and wash our feet in Machrie burn,—
Refreshed, pass Auchingallan, Auchincar,
Their Monoliths and Cairns, remains of war;
Till Duggery Lodge reminds of modern days,
Ease, elegance, pride, sloth, and wasteful ways;
A weary tramp 'mong boulders, gravel, stones,
Beside the sea, till Imacher atones,
With rest and food obtained in Farm-stead Inn;
Again we spurt White Farland-point to win,
Next Pirn-Mill with its boats and fishermen,
On past Penrioch, Thundergay, and then
Upon the rocks we sat, and in the tide,
We bathe our burning, weary feet, beside
The Areverga Church and burying ground:
Beyond the Church, 'neath Limestone Cliff, we found
Where winds the road, round by dark Catacol,
A spring, *the best* I think for thirsty soul,
We ever drank (*with one exception,*)—quite
Invigorating, thrilling with delight.
Oh! here the scenery is wildly grand,
With mountain, glen, and sea, so close at hand.
Across Kilbrannan Sound the Cantyre Coast
Is seen, and hills of Galloway are lost
To sight; where sea and sky in distance meet
'Neath sunset clouds which make the scene complete.
Round one more Point, we fair Lochranza see;
Reach Hillside Cottage—and at eight have tea;
Hunger long felt doth dull the appetite,—
That may be so, but ours is keen to-night:
We do enjoy and praise the homely spread
Of herrings fried, to tea and toasted bread.
This done, we rest our weary limbs awhile,
Then ramble round, 'mong deepening shades, a mile,
And halt entranced, where, bathed in moonlight sheen,
'Ye Castle Olde' stands 'mid romantic scene;

And as on fancy's wing I grandly soared,
Peopling with hunters, king, and festive board;
Friend James, with hearty laugh, kept on averring,
'Ay! Ay! but no Lochfyne *pen-osh-les* herring.'
But Morpheus soon all roving thought beguiles,
For to-day we've travelled thirty Arran miles.
At six, reluctantly we *dejeuner*;
By seven o'clock we tread our weary way
Of uphill road, through dark glen Chalmidel:
One ling'ring backward look we take—the spell
Is broken by the moor-fowls' scream, or laugh
So harsh, where bees the heath-bells' honey quaff.
We gain the top,—*lave, but drink little*, from
Yon wayside stream, that trickles o'er the dome
Of rock, half hid 'mong ferns, wild flowers, and moss.
Down hill we go, until at length, across
A dreary stretch of mountain, moor, and fen,
We mark the sea, and lo! the Sannox glen
Is opening on our right, in grandeur bold,—
Majestically, its charms unfold,
Until we tread the wooded level way
That leads on past the winding gravelly bay,
Beside whose shores some granite boulders lie;
A Rocking-stone quite near the road, we try
In vain to move—'A joke perhaps,' we say,—
Or possibly our strength has *walked* away,
Our guide-book *said it*—try it if you can?
If ere 'twas done, 'twas by a Hielan' man.
A lovely walk, ozone and zephyr blest,
Leads past the Corrie, that sweet dell, caressed
By Nature in perpetual summer mood;
Tropical plants, here, years outside have stood;
Protected by grand Goatfell's towering crest,
Defying, lifting from North, East, and West,
The tempest's power,—and as close by its base
We ramble, ever and anon we raise
Our eyes to view the mountain's shaggy sides;
We mark some heath-clad water course where glides
The glancing streamlet, foaming, dashing o'er
'Mong granite blocks and time-worn rocks, with roar
And hiss,—like echoes from yon stormy deep,
Whose treacherous waves seem now for aye asleep.
A walk,—so sheltered—for six miles or more
We follow speedily along the shore,

Till Merkland Point is reached; here often when
The gloaming shades brood over mount and glen,
You'll see the lonely heron sit, or fly
With lazy wing, and strange old-manish cry
Among the rocks; or hear the sea-gull's scream,
And plover's pipe, where restless wavelets gleam.
Fond memory lingers then o'er scenes gone by,
Full fondly—but we now must haste and try
For Brodick Pier before yon steamer comes
That brings some friends beloved from other homes;
A passing glance or so we only give
To Castle and its splendid grounds, where live
At times those noble Lords, and sporting Dukes,
So often pictured out so grand in books,
And novels' trashy pages,—barren, bare;
They're scarcely human,—gifts and virtues rare
Adorn their every act in print and letter,
Till,—well—ah! yes!—you know them better.
See there's the *Brodick Castle* steaming in
Close to the Pier,—so we must spurt and win
Our goal, or friends may disappointed gaze
For faces dear among the assembling blaze
Of many coloured coats, and summer dresses;
White, black, and *red*;—no! gold and amber tresses.
Once more we climb the winding, shady way,
Towards Strathwheelan, from whose slopes, the Bay
Superbly grand looks as it lies below,
The fairest piece of scenery I know.
Talk not of Naples, or of foreign lands;
When bathed in sunny smile, unrivalled stands
This treasured scene. And now though tired we're in it,
Four and a quarter hours, timed to a minute,
Since starting out to-day, and sixteen miles
Behind us lie; we rest while beauty smiles,
Welcoming home. Our happy ramble's o'er,—
Enshrined, methinks, in memory evermore.

William Brown Smith *The World Without and Within and other poems* (Saltcoats: Archibald Wallace, 1887)

Lamlash Churchyard

C.T. Borrie, 1882

An old Stewarton lady, with an old privileged handmaid, one day visited Lamlash Churchyard. While resting on a headstone the mistress, captivated by the surrounding hills and the quiet well-kept 'God's acre', said, 'This is a far nicer place to be buried in than oor place at hame that's owergrown wi' nettles and covered wi' broken bottles; I would like to lie here, it's sae quait and bonnie.' 'No me, mistress,' said the servant; 'I want to lie in oor ain kirkyard among kent folk.' 'It's a dull gruesome place,' replied the mistress; 'this is far afore't.' 'It's a' weel eneuch whan ye're lyin', nae doot,' said the handmaiden boldly, 'but what wull't be whan ye rise, wi' nane but strangers about ye yatterin Gaelic in your lug, and you no kennin' a word they say? I wonder to hear ye, mistress. I'll lie at hame, and then I'll ken the company when I'm waukened.'

C. St Marketto (C.T. Borrie) *Trial Trip of the S.S. 'St. George'* (Blackie, 1882)

The Kye Song

Alexander Mac Lachlan, 1888

Tune—'Prutchie Kye'

Will ye gang, oh will ye gang
 Wi' me to seek the kye?
Will ye gang, oh will ye gang,
 For the night is drawing nigh.
Will ye gang, oh will ye gang
 Wi' me to seek the kye?
They hae strayed the hills amang,
 And the night is drawing nigh.

Will ye gang, oh will ye gang
 Wi' me to seek the kye?
They hae strayed the hills amang,
 And the night is drawing nigh!
Far up the hill they've gane,
 Owre by Goat Fell sae high,
An' I'm eerie a' my lane
 At night to seek the kye!

Will ye gang, oh will ye gang
    Wi' me to seek the kye?
I hae wander'd a' night lang,
    An' I canna find the kye!
I hae sought the braes owre there,
    Whare 'fore I've fand them lie,
An' on yon heather muir,
    But I canna find the kye!

Chorus
Prutchie, prutchie, prutchie, kye!
    Prutchie, prutchie, prutchie! cry!
Pruite, pruite, pruite, pruite, try, oh try!
    Tweet, tweet, tweet! to find thae kye!
Prutchie, prutchie, prutchie, kye!
    Prutchie, prutchie, prutchie, cry!
Pruite, pruite, pruite, pruite! I will try—
    Tweet, tweet, tweet! to find your kye!

I am frichtet for the deer!
    Oh there they're! come awa!
Their rairin now, ye hear,
    I canna gang ava!
Within yon wood sae mirk,
    An' 'bout yon gloomy glen,
There are *speerits* said to lurk,
    An' I canna gang my lane.

Prutchie, prutchie, prutchie, kye!
    I'll maybe gar them steer!
Oh yonder hear them cry!
    Oh no! it is the deer!
How near they are to us,
    How swiftly they do fly!
High up the glen they rus'!
    I wish I had thae kye.

I gaed wi' her thro' glens,
    Owre mosses, muirs, an' hills;
Thro' flaggs and ferny fens,
    An' lap wi' her the rills;
Owre granite rocks an' stanes,
    In night-black eerie wuds,
An' ghaist-behaunted dens
    Whare down the torrent thuds!

A' owre the place we gaed
  By hill, wood, road, an' shore,
Whare she thought they had strayed,
  Or had been fand afore;
As far as the dark Moal-Donn,
  An' by the Meikle Stane,
An' owre the Muirland lone,
  Cross Corrie and Eas Bàn!

Alexander Mac Lachlan *Songs of Arran* (Edinburgh, 1889)

Lodgings at Arran
Alexander G. Murdoch, 1888

Tammy Lawbrod, a tailor chappie, an' I gaed doon to Arran last Fair Setterday to spend a week's holidays. We had a picturesque week o't, an' no mistake! We had often heard the Island o' Arran spoken aboot as a grand place for pickin' up health. The air was sae wonderfu' fresh there, an' the saut water sae strong, that the folks said ye cood thrive finely there, an' even grow fat on plain tatties and herrin', mornin', noon, an' nicht, washt doon wi' a jugfu' o' soor mulk. Oor livin' at Arran was, therefore, likely to prove very cheap. But, if the livin' was likely to prove cheap, the lodgin's turned oot a saut enough concern, I can tell ye!

Lodgin's at Arran! D'ye ken what that means? It means oftener than no' twa pounds a week for a hen hoose, wi' six or eicht in the bed, a coo's byre next door, an' the rain comin' through the roof! Talk aboot gaun abroad to see the picturesque in life! Gang doon to Arran at the Gleska Fair-holiday time, an' ye'll never need to gang farrer to see mair. Weel, we hadna jist exactly six in oor bed—Tammy Lawbrod an' I; but oor room was quite remarkable for the want o' room. To begin wi', the wee microscopic bed we slept in had obviously been made for the accommodation o' some Italian organ-grinder's monkey in bad health. It was sae sma' that Tammy an' I had, yin micht almost say, to examine it wi' oor specks on! It was a fine tak'-in, that same furnished room. We saw it advertised in the Gleska papers as a

FURNISHED ROOM TO LET AT ARRAN,
Suitable for two bachelor gentlemen; fine sea-view; garden at the back; every convenience; own key; terms moderate! Address—Mrs McTavish, Brodick.

The advertisement, ye'll notice, was very nicely worded, an' was fitted to draw like a mustard poultice. It drew Tammy Lawbrod an' mysel' a' the

78

Goatfell and Brodick Sands by F. Noel-Paton (Art Journal, July 1885)

way doon to Arran jist like that! (snapping finger and thumb). We wrote doon for it at yince, an' engaged it for eicht days, without seein' it; the advertisement, alang wi' Mrs McTavish, was sae fu' o' promise. Talk aboot buyin' a pig in a pock! It was waur than even that, it was aboot as bad as a man tryin' to read the papers wi' the specks on the back o' his heid! Brodick's no a big place; but we had, nevertheless, some difficulty in findin' oot Mrs McTavish.

'De ye ken whaur Mrs McTavish bides?' I speired at a native, a wild-lookin' man wi' red hair, tartan troosers, and a squint e'e.

'Faur daes she leeve?' replied the Celt, 'tell me faur she stays?' 'That's what I'm wantin' to ken, man,' said I.

'So wass me,' answered the Celt, with a wild grin.

'Can ye no' tell me whaur Mrs McTavish bides?' I yince mair asked him.

'Wass you come a' ta way doon from Klasko to see Mrs McTavish?' inquisitively replied the Celt.

'Tuts, man, d'ye no' ken whaur Mrs McTavish bides, I'm speirin' ye— yes or no'?' 'Mrs McTavish! Mrs McTavish!' ruminated the Celt, 'fat Mrs McTavish wass she bee wantin'?'

'Mrs McTavish wha lets the summer lodgin's,' I answered.

'Hump!' replied the Celt with a shrug, 'efery Mrs McTavish, an' Mrs Macfarlanes, an' Mrs Macdougalls, an' efery other housewife on ta island keeps twa or four lodgers whateffer, an' twice as more too.'

Brodick's no a big place, however, as ye a' ken, an' I fand oot oor identical landlady before lang. She was standin' in the doorway lookin' oot for oor comin'. We had passed her, back an' forrit, half-a-dizzen times before we ever even suspected that she was Mrs McTavish, or that the hut she occupied was the 'Cottage at Arran' we had seen described in that highly romantic and drawing advertisement.

The 'cottage' was a yae-story concern, and looked a sort o' twa-hunder-year-auld shepherd's hut or dowg-hoose, tooken doon, holus bolus, frae the hillside somewhaur, an' set on the edge o' the road as a protest against all modern ideas of ordinary taste and comfort. The 'garden' at the back was a genuine cabbage yin! Mrs McTavish was a pure native o' the island. She snuffed, wore mutches an' specks, an' spoke a limited quantity of English, interfused wi' an unlimited quantity o' unpronounceable Gaelic.

Beyond an' above a' that, Mrs McTavish was a very thrifty, economical woman. Her hoose consisted o' a but-an'-ben, or, to phrase the thing more genteelly, a room an' a kitchen. She kept a coo, and a lot o' cocks an' hens in the hoose, forbye her lodgers. The hens had the best o' it. They had, at a' hours, an' on a' occasions, the unqualified run o' the hoose, an' between their ceaseless cackle, the cocks' fearful crawin', an' the fine, fresh smell o' the auld coo, tethered at the faur-awa en' o' the kitchen bed, the place, mornin' noon, an' nicht, was remarkably fu' o' the very strongest country odours and associations.

Talk aboot the picturesque in foreign travel! For a genuine e'e-opener, try Arran. Mrs McTavish's yae-room-an'-kitchen concern in Arran was a whussler, I can tell ye! It was the most musical, as weel as the most diversified, lodgin's I ever stayed in. As early as fowr in the mornin', it was cockie-leerie-law! in yer sleepin' lugs frae the tane or the tither o' the twa cocks; a' the forenoon it was moo-oo! frae the auld coo in the kitchen; while mornin', noon, and nicht, it was naething but clack, clack, clack! frae the twa-and-twenty hens that roosted singly or in pairs in a' parts o' the hoose.

But we had a waur experience than a' that—Tammy Lawbrod an' I. The hoose was a fine airy yin, the roof was thatched wi' straw, an' had numerous keek-holes in't, thro' which the daylicht peeped like wee stars. This was a' very fine sae lang as the weather kept dry. But a break in the barometer took place yae nicht suddenly, aboot fowr in the mornin', an' the scene was changed, as the poet says. That mornin' I was waukened oot o' a deep sleep wi' Tammy Lawbrod dunchin' me on the shoother wi' his elbow. I started, an' looked aboot me.

'What's the maitter, Tammy?' I asked.

'The maitter! d'ye no' see what's up?' he asked, 'why, it's poorin' o' rain in here, an' I'm jist thinkin' it wad be better for us baith to get up an' gang ootside till it taks aff! This is fine, lively, picturesque lodgin's we've cam' to, an' no mistake!'

'Dook yer heid under the blankets till the rain's aff,' quo' I, wi' a laugh, for I coodna help laughin' at the oddity o' the situation, badly as we were in for't.

'Nae yise,' replied Tammy, 'the blankets 'ill be wat thro' in twa ticks; the rain's already lyin' in wee pools on the tap o' them! It's an umbrella we're sairly needin', I'm thinkin'.

'The very thing!' I joyfully exclaimed, an' afore ye cou'd say Jake Robinson, I had jumpit oot the bed, seized my auld umbrella, an' getting yince mair laid doon in bed, flapp't it up abune oor twa heids, to save oorsel's frae the rain that was skytin' doon on us frae the dreepin' roof!

An' for twa lang hours we lay in the bed there, wi' oor nichtcaps drawn doon owre oor twa lugs, an' the umbrella spread owre oor heids, a grand specimen o' the picturesque in life—and lodgin's in Arran! I kenna how auld Mrs McTavish got on in the kitchen that rainy nicht; but I ken that some o' the cocks an' hens had to hide for shelter ere mornin' below the chairs an' tables!

Folks ha'e different ideas o' hoo to spend a holiday; but I'll say this much, if ye want a new experience in life spend a week in Arran. But for ony sake dinna gang there withoot takin' wi' ye an ample supply o' waterproof, along wi' a fine big bed-room UMBRELLA!

Alexander G. Murdoch (1843-1891) *Scotch Readings*. 2nd series (Glasgow: Thomas Morison, 1888)

The Arran Murder

The Scotsman and Glasgow Herald, 1889

On Saturday evening [9 November], after a long and patient trial, John Watson Laurie was convicted of the murder of Edwin Rose in Arran, in July last…. The story is one that, if it were made the plot of a novel, would be regarded as highly sensational, if it was not also regarded as in the last degree improbable.

Edwin Rose was clerk to a builder in London named Goodman. He was a highly intelligent young fellow, careful, honest, thoroughly trusted. Mr Goodman had a brother, a clergyman, who had come to Rothesay to spend his holiday. It was at his suggestion that Rose determined to go up to Rothesay for his holiday. He left London in the first week of July, and went to the Glenburn Hydropathic establishment. John Watson Laurie was a patternmaker employed at the Springburn Works in Glasgow. He had a reputation for being fond of dress, and of aping men in a higher position in life than that in which he was placed. On the 6th of July he had gone on a holiday to Bute, and on that day, calling himself Annandale, he took lodgings with a Mrs Currie at Port Bannatyne. On the 12th of July a party of friends from the Glenburn Hydropathic went for a day's excursion to Arran. Rose was one of the party. Laurie, calling himself Annandale, was also on board the steamer. In the course of the day's trip they struck up a sort of acquaintanceship, and, on the return of the steamer to Rothesay, Rose took Annandale to the hydropathic establishment and introduced him to persons staying there as his friend. There is some evidence that one or two of the friends of Rose cautioned him against Laurie, whose manners did not impress them. These cautions, however, had no effect, and the two men seem to have planned that they would go the next day for a short stay in Arran. Accordingly, on the 13th of July, a Saturday, they travelled together to Arran, and took lodgings in the house of Mrs Walker at Brodick. They occupied the same room, and in all respects acted as if in close friendship. They strolled about the island on the Saturday evening and throughout the Sunday, but made it known that they had resolved to ascend Goatfell on the Monday. That Monday was the 15th of July. They started in the afternoon for their walk up. They were met by people who knew them, and they were accompanied part of the way by others, with whom they entered into conversation. The summit of Goatfell was reached, and shortly after six o'clock they were seen standing on a boulder, Laurie pointing in a particular direction, as if to indicate a return path. This direction was not that of the ordinary ascent and descent. From that moment Rose was never again seen alive. One witness swears that he saw Laurie coming out of Glen Sannox about half-past nine in the evening—more than three hours after he and Rose had been seen on the summit; and a policeman who had walked the distance between the summit and the place where Laurie was seen stated that he did so in an hour and forty minutes. Subsequently, Laurie went into a hotel at Corrie, and there got drink at the bar. The next that was seen of him, so far as the evidence shows, was the following morning when he went on board a steamer, carrying with him two bags, and wearing a hat which undoubtedly had belonged to Rose. How he became possessed of these things was clear enough. After Mrs Walker had gone to bed, neither of her lodgers having come home, Laurie must have entered the house and taken away not only what belonged to himself, but almost everything that belonged to Rose. It is not denied that he did this. He went to Glasgow, returned to Rothesay again, spent the rest of his holiday there, then went to Glasgow on the 22nd of July, returned to work at Springburn, remained there till the 30th of July, and on the 31st of that month left his employment and began a series of wanderings which took him to Liverpool and other places, and ended in his capture as the suspected murderer of Rose.

Meantime, Mrs Walker had made known the fact that her lodgers had disappeared. Apparently, however, this disappearance of summer lodgers in Arran is not so uncommon as to create interest or anxiety. It simply means that some honest person has not received the rent that was her due. Thus it was that in Arran no particular anxiety seems to have been felt; but in London, Rose's friends, not hearing from him, became extremely anxious, and made inquiries in various directions. His brother came up to Bute and on to Arran, and there learned not only that Edwin Rose had never been known to return from his ascent of Goatfell, but that the man called Annandale, who had accompanied him in his ascent, had been seen afterwards. A search was instituted, and for a week all the glens and corries of Goatfell were scoured for traces of the missing man. At last, on the 4th of August, his body was found by Francis Logan. It was practically hidden away under a huge boulder, and heavy stones had been heaped upon it and in front of it. The pockets of the dead man were turned inside out. The head had been beaten to a jelly, corruption had set in to a frightful extent, and identification would have been all but impossible except for the clothes that were worn. A cap which had belonged to Rose was found in a stream close by with a stone placed over it. There were no traces of blood in the neighbourhood, and nothing to indicate any struggle. Those who found the body came at once to the conclusion, a most natural one in the circumstances, that a murder had been committed, and suspicion fell upon Annandale. It will be seen that the evidence against him, so far, was of a strong presumptive character. He was the last man seen with Rose before the latter's death. He was twice as long getting from the summit of Goatfell to the Corrie Hotel as he would have been if he had come straight down. He went to the lodgings he and Rose had occupied, and he carried off Rose's belongings. Subsequently, when he had learned that a search was being made for the body of Rose, he left his employment in Glasgow and went away, evading the search that soon began to be made for him.

In all this it will be obvious that the connection between Annandale or Laurie and Rose is completely proved. They were seen together on the summit of the hill; they were never seen together afterwards. Rose was found dead. Laurie behaved in a most suspicious manner. No one could doubt that Rose's death had been caused by violence. The theory of the Crown was that he had been knocked down by a blow with a heavy stone, and that his head had then been battered into a jelly; after which his pockets had been rifled, and the body had been placed where it was subsequently found. The Crown insisted that this had all been done by Laurie. The theory of the defence was that the two men parted at the top of Goatfell; that Rose had fallen over a precipice; that his body had been found by some one, who had robbed him of all he had, and had then put the body where it was found. The medical evidence on the side of the Crown was that such injuries as had been received could not have been caused by a fall over a precipice. The medical evidence for the defence, based upon the statements of the condition of the body, was that the injuries could have been caused by a fall. In effect this was the point the jury had to decide. Laurie might be a scoundrel. He might have robbed his companion. He might have told innumerable falsehoods, but all these things would be compatible with his innocence of murder. Nay, there was another possibility that might have been taken into account, though it does not seem to have been urged by counsel for the defence. Rose might have slipped and fallen, being stunned or perhaps killed in the fall; and then Laurie, horrified at this accident, might have yielded to the temptation to rob him. If this theory were the correct one, it would be impossible for the jury to find Laurie guilty of murder. Not only was this defence not urged; but it was insisted by the Dean of Faculty that it would have been impossible for Laurie to have placed the body where it was found, and that it must have been so placed by at least two people, passers-by. The Lord Justice-Clerk, in summing up, cautioned the jury as to the medical evidence, pointing out the difference that must exist between evidence given after actual inspection of the body and what may be called theoretical evidence, given on the reports of those who had seen the body. No doubt the jury gave full effect to this advice. They found the theory for the defence too hard for belief. In the first place, if Laurie had parted from Rose on the summit of Goatfell, and had not seen him afterwards, how did it happen that he took first of all a much longer time than was necessary to descend the mountain, and that afterwards he went to the lodgings he and Rose had occupied, and carried off Rose's belongings? He could not get away from the island until the next morning. If, then, he was innocent of all knowledge of Rose's death, he would never have thought of taking away Rose's belongings from the lodgings, because he would have expected him to return home some time during the night. If his action in entering Mrs Walker's house surreptitiously and leaving it surreptitiously with the things belonging to Rose does not prove his guilt, it throws the strongest possible suspicion upon him. All his subsequent actions might be accounted for by a fear of being misjudged, but the one action that could not be so interpreted was his robbery of Rose's luggage at Mrs Walker's. No ordinary mind will doubt that when he took Rose's bag away he knew that Rose was dead, and, if he knew that this was the case, the theory of the defence is thoroughly broken down. It was said that none of the articles known to be in the possession of Rose when he ascended Goatfell had been found or seen in the possession of Laurie. This is literally true; but things were found in Laurie's possession that there is reason to believe Rose would be carrying in his pockets on that fatal day. This, however, is a matter of small importance. The whole case practically turns upon very narrow points. Was Rose murdered? The jury have believed that he was, and no one who reads the evidence can doubt that, although he might have been injured previously by a fall, he was maltreated afterwards, and this maltreatment would have been sufficient to cause death. Who, then, murdered him? The actions of Laurie point to him as the culprit. If he had known nothing of Rose's death, he could not have done what he did that night. It is difficult, then, to see how the jury could rightly have returned any other verdict. Short of direct evidence of the crime, such as that of a witness who saw it committed, there could not be a stronger case than is made out against the wretched prisoner by the strong circumstantial evidence that has been adduced.

Scotsman 11 November 1889

Letters to the Editor of the *Glasgow Herald*

20 Leven Street, Pollokshields
21st November 1889

Sir,—The varied opinions that have been ventilated through your columns regarding the unfortunate man Laurie may be said to be a reflex of public opinion. The exhaustive letter of Dr Adams of yesterday is certainly of considerable significance. That a medical gentleman should give in such a clear and forcible manner his positive assurance that all the injuries as detailed in evidence could and might be produced by accidental falling surely ought to cause further inquiry by the Home Secretary. That such an accident might take place the following will place beyond dispute:—A number of years ago I was investigating the character of the Arran granite, and went by the Campbeltown steamer to Lochranza in order to get a transverse examination of the island from Lochranza to Brodick. When approaching the north end of the island, a gentleman from Glasgow asked me if I knew the road to Brodick. I gave him the necessary information, and told him that I was going to Brodick through the range of mountains. He insisted to be allowed to accompany me. I made him aware of the dangerous path I was going by.

He came with me. We got to the summit of the Suide-Fergus range, on the north side of Glen Sannox, opposite to where Mr Rose's body was found. We got the setting sun from that altitude. The sight was grand beyond description. Whether it was the grandeur of the sight, or the altitude, or physical inability, I do not know; but during the few minutes we were there I accidentally turned round to pass a remark to my friend, and found him swooning, and about to fall over a deep precipice, and had I not been able to save him he would have fallen over a cliff of great depth, and certainly would have met his death. I was the only person he was seen with during the greater part of the day. The shepherd met us on our way up the mountain, consequently had an accident occurred it might have been asserted that he had met his death by foul means. I had no one to exonerate me from blame, and might have been put to no end of trouble. Now, sir, regarding Laurie's movements I have nothing to say. It would be satisfactory if he would make some statement. But from the above it will be inferred that it is within the range of probability that an accident did take place. The gentleman that I saved is still living, and no doubt this letter will recall to him the circumstances above related.—I am, etc.,

James Thomson

Blairbeth, Rutherglen
21st November 1889

Sir,—I have been greatly exercised in my mind in considering all the points and theories that have been advanced...acquitting or condemning John Watson Laurie.... From the very outset I have held to a strong, unaccountable conviction that Laurie never committed any murder—that death to Rose was the result of an accident, and in no way attributable to Laurie. I have never changed my mind. I said then, and now I know it to be true, that Laurie is not altogether of sound mind or judgment, or one likely to act in any dilemma like the common race of mankind. I believe Rose to have fallen from the top; and when Laurie discovered that he was really dead, he then and there conceived the insane idea of hiding him up or building him in out of sight once and for ever, in foolish fear lest he should be blamed, and simply took Rose's possessions, not for their intrinsic value, but to blot out any trace, and thus prevent identity should the body ever be found. Insane, inordinate vanity enabled him to wear the clothes afterwards, but he never, certainly in my opinion, murdered Rose to possess them.

On reading Dr Adams's letter in the *Herald*, I was very much struck by his remarks regarding Rose, which bear a strong likeness to an incident that came under my own notice. And, however much I would shrink from publicity, nevertheless, if what I shall herein state as corroborative proof of his statement should in any way save Laurie from the scaffold, I shall not have written in vain.

In May, 1875, three young men made the ascent of Goatfell. They were students, two divinity and one medical. The day was intensely cold, and the Fell was ever and anon enveloped in white mist. When half-way up they considered much whether, on account of their unfortunate choice of a day, it would not be advisable to descend. But, as it had been a long-planned expedition, they all agreed to go up to the very top. On reaching the summit, and while standing at a very narrow pass, they were again enshrouded in the white mist, when suddenly and most unexpectedly one of the three cried out as if he were going to fall over, his nose commenced to bleed profusely, his brain swam with an indescribable cold, numb, and reeling or giving-way sensation, coupled with a dread horror of falling over.

I was married to that same young man in September, 1876, the year after, and when passing through Brodick a few days after our marriage I made the observation, on viewing Goatfell, 'that it would be rather strange if we did not make it a visit.' He asked if I very much desired to make the ascent. I replied, 'Well, yes, I think so.' Something in his tone struck me vaguely, and I looked up and said: 'I rather think you don't fancy going,' and with a look of dread, which I often recall, he said: 'I can never think of standing up there on that summit but with a great sense of horror, like what I felt that day.' My husband died two years afterwards—20th September, 1878—very suddenly, and apparently without cause, his heart being sound and his general health good.

Had it not been for my reading Dr Adams's letter in your paper, I had not the most remote knowledge that I possessed any information likely to throw light on this subject, and would deem it a sin to withhold anything that may free the poor erring youth. And doubtless as he was then, so is he still, afraid to tell the simple truth, believing it would only be regarded as an idle tale, or a pure fabrication. Although no sane person could approve or imitate Laurie's course of procedure, nevertheless, as he is, it is cruel and unjust to judge him by other men, and if my solution of the matter be correct, it exonerates him (being as he is) from all blame.—I am, etc.,

L.M. Dunbar

Reprinted in: *Trial of John Watson Laurie (The Arran Murder)* edited by William Roughead (Edinburgh and London: William Hodge, 1932) (Notable British Trials Series)

The Kirn-Supper
Charles E. Hall, 1893

The night was dark, and lights were twinkling in the village inn at Lag. Something unwonted was astir, for the windows were unusually illuminated. Bernard Drake, who had walked over from his tent, for any letters that might be lying for him at the inn, was struck, not only by the unusual radiance proceeding from every aperture, but also by the sounds of revelry emanating from within. There was a regular succession of noises, like persons bouncing on a floor, to the accompaniment of mirth and music. Pipe, tabor, and fiddle were hard at work, the performers playing reels and strathspeys with all their might and main. Bernard could not at first understand the cause of this merry-making, but presently it dawned upon him that the natives were celebrating what in Scotland is called the *Kirn*, and in England, *Harvest-Home*; an annual feast of ingathering, common, under different names, in every land. Only that same afternoon, while walking through a cornfield, he had witnessed a quaint old custom, almost obsolete everywhere but in Arran and some of the islands of the Hebrides, called 'Crying the Mare'. The *Mare* is the last handful of corn, which is tied up and erected, while the reapers, one after another, throw their sickles at it, to cut it down. Then they form themselves into two bands, and commence the following

Lagg Hotel

88

dialogue in loud shouts, or rather in a kind of chant, at the top of their voice. First band: *I have her, I have her, I have her.* (Every sentence is shouted three times.) Second: *What hast thee? What hast thee? What hast thee?* First: *A mare, a mare, a mare!* Second: *Whose is her? Whose is her? Whose is her?* First: A.B.'s (naming their master, whose corn is all cut). Second: *Where shall we send her?* etc. First: To C.D. (naming some neighbour whose corn is still standing). And the whole concludes with a joyous shout by the united bands, while a messenger is despatched with the *mare* to the next farmer who happens to be still at work upon his crops.

Bernard had been amused at this piece of rustic pleasantry, and was ready to join in the merriment of the *Kirn-Supper* at the inn. By this time the actual feast was over, haggis and venison being all consumed. Boards and benches had been removed, and when Bernard entered the long, low, gaily-decorated room, a large space had been cleared for the dancers. Coming out of the darkness, he was at first almost blinded by the lights to which, however, he grew accustomed, when he was able to take in the characteristic features of the lively scene around him....

It seemed rather an anomaly at this harvest-feast, that most of the participants in it were fisher-folk, rather than agricultural labourers. The festival was evidently a general one. All sorts and conditions of people were there. The Rev. Daniel Miller and Malvina Fergusson, who had come as Mrs Gillies' guests, were present; and Mrs Penworthy, as an inmate of the house, tall, prim, and proper, with her side-curls stiffer and bristlier than ever, had deigned to patronise the humble amusements of the villagers. All the neighbours, old and young, seemed to have dropped in. The miller and the blacksmith and the general shopkeeper, in their Sunday coats, with their wives and daughters, beribboned and adorned in airy drapery. Fishermen and ploughmen; sailors and rustics;—a motley crew.

Beakers of beer were in great request, and on a table in one corner of the room stood an immense bowl of whisky-punch. Jenny McCallum was here, there, and everywhere; now waiting on the guests, now joining in a Highland fling, or a country dance. Old Duncan Macdougal, too, was there; spinning yarns by the score, and giving an occasional hand with the pipes, on which he was a proficient player. He it was who was the first to notice the new-comer.

'Why, Mester Drake, ye are recht welcome to our *kirn*,' said the brawny fisherman, thrusting forth a paw much the colour of a badger's back, and of the most portentous dimensions.

'Wha is't tou's gotten thire, Duncan, lad?' cried half-a-score of voices, while all eyes were turned on Bernard.

'A braw loon, I can tell ye,' shouted Duncan. 'It's him as owns the tent awa' doon by the shoor yonder. It's him as maks picters on the braes.'

'Ay, lad, I ken him by his velvet jacket. He's a gentle chap, I reckon, by his looks.'

'Gentle or no, he's wilcome to the *kirn*. But where hae ye been, Mester Drake, to miss the supper?'

'I knew nothing of the supper, unfortunately, or should have come earlier,' explained Bernard.

'Well, here's t'ye, noo, any way,' said Duncan, handing him a glass of punch, and draining one himself.

After that, the young artist claimed Jenny McCallum as a partner, and they tripped away together to the music of Duncan's pipes.

The dances were, of course, the Scottish jigs and reels, and 'twasome dances', with a schottische, or hornpipe, or strathspey for interlude; and any deficiency in grace on the part of the performers was atoned for by correctness of ear, vigour and decision of step, and a considerable display of agility. Bernard Drake quite enjoyed the rustic revel, and danced so well as to call forth encomiums from the onlookers, who expressed themselves in such remarks as, 'Weel dune, gentle chap, yet!' and 'Nay, but he con foot it, sure. Thire's waur dancin' tha' that e'en i' Glasgie.' Several of the younger women began to throw jealous looks on Jenny, and would have liked Bernard for a partner, too, but Mrs McCallum herself, a buxom dame, the mistress of the feast, whose dancing days were not yet over, asked him for the next reel, a hostess's privilege.

'Why, Mistress McCallum, you do me too much honour,' expostulated Bernard, with elaborate courtesy.

'Nay, but I would like to take the floor for a dance or twa wi' such a brave young gentleman.'

'And what's to come of me, mither?' said Jenny, pouting.

'Come o' thee?' quoth the dame; 'mishanter on the bold face o' ye! ye would tire out the haill o' your partners afore ye'd dune wi' 'em. Jist wait on thi' mither's guests, and be a gude girl, d'ye hear?'

'I am a gude girl, I'm a varra, varra gude girl,' retorted Jenny, with another pout, walking away to replenish with ale an empty beaker for one of the guests.

Just when Bernard was about to lead Mrs McCallum forth for the dance, he espied, for the first time, Mr Miller and Malvina, who had been sitting quietly with Mrs Gillies in a corner of the room, looking on at the festivities. He was so astonished and delighted, that he felt inclined to drop his partner's arm and go up to them at once.

But Mrs McCallum stuck to him like a leech, and the rest of the dancers were waiting for the two of them to lead off the reel. He was only brought to his senses by Duncan Macdougal, who gave him a friendly slap on the shoulder, saying:

'The lasses are a' waiting, Mr Drake. To the floor—to the floor, and let them see how ye can fling.'

'Ay, lad,' murmured Mrs McCallum, 'ye dinna mean to say Jenny has tired ye sae airly. Ye seem unca sune weary. Better the nag that ambles a' the day, than him that makes a brattle for a mile, and then's dune wi' the road.'

So Bernard, without more ado, but with one last glance in the direction of Malvina, who recognised him and gave him a gracious smile of welcome, seized hold of his willing partner's hand, and the two took their places in the dance. Jenny's mother frisked about as nimbly as Jenny herself, snapping her fingers in the air, whooping the war-cry of the reel, and bounding from the floor like an india-rubber ball. Bernard was much less energetic, but apparently acquitted himself to his partner's satisfaction, although he was longing to be quit of her. At length the good woman was out of breath and could dance no more. Bernard, rejoicing at his release, led her to a seat.

'Why, lad,' she exclaimed, panting, 'I am sair forfoughen! I think ye hae been amaist the death o' me.'

'Nay, Mrs McCallum, it has not been my doing, surely. You dance too well, and foot it too merrily, for such a poor partner as myself.'

'Hout wi' your fleeching. Why, man, ye're prime at it!'

Just then another young fellow came up to claim the hostess for the next dance, and Bernard was able to effect his escape. He lost no time in hurrying to the corner of the room where his friends were seated.

'Oh, Mr Drake, you have come at the right moment,' said Miss Fergusson, shaking hands with him. 'Uncle Dan can't tell me what the word *kirn* actually means, and even Mrs Gillies, here, Scotchwoman though she is, pretends she does not know. Can *you* help me?'

'That I can,' answered Bernard, sitting down beside them. 'It means a churn in English; and this annual festival is called the *Kirn* or *Kirn-Supper*, from the churn of cream which used to be presented on the occasion. Whether the custom is quite obsolete here, I don't know myself, but we'll ask Mrs McCallum presently. At all events, the name survives. You have a prettier title for the affair in England; you call this sort of thing a *harvest-home*, do you not?'

Charles E. Hall *An Ancient Ancestor: A Tale of Three Weeks* (London: Skeffington & Son, 1893)

Characters

George Milner, 1894

Saturday, August 2

And now, round the corner of the house, there comes an old friend, John Campbell, the 'Provost' of Corrie, as, with good-natured banter, he is usually called. Although he carries upon his shoulders the weight of more than eighty years, this last one seems to have added little to his burden. He steps forward as if he were pacing the unsteady deck of a lugger; and, putting his rough brown hand over his eyes, he looks round with an air of responsible authority upon the little hamlet and the wide sea as one who should say—'stands Corrie where it did?' After salutations he opens out upon me quite at random, and as if we had parted not eleven months ago, but at sundown yesterday—The ministers are a' wrang in their theology; jist blind leaders o' the blind, for not the one half o' them have been properly through the colleges. Why, with the Auld Testament in his haund he could pit them through their catechism hissel, and mak them a' flee before him—puir creatures as they are. In his opinion the body politic, no less than the ecclesiastic, is in a parlous condition. These workin' folk have sent a' things tapsalteerie wi' their strikes and their high wages. When he was in the quarry he was weel content with his twa shillings a day; and the best mason among them a' got no more than three. An' what then; they were better off a lang sight than they are now.

*

Thursday, August 7
Among the characters of Lamlash is Sandy McGlosher. Sandy is a fisherman and a boatman, and has a thriving trade. All through the winter months he fishes hard, and never tastes whisky; but as soon as summer brings visitors, Sandy is sober no more. It is whisky, whisky, all the day long. Last night, after eleven o'clock, a splash in the water was heard by a casual passer-by. Sandy had rolled off the pier, and had a narrow escape of his life. He was drawn in by one foot—a mere floating log. 'Well, Sandy,' we said to him, 'it was well you were picked up last night.'

'Oh, don't believe it, gentlemen, don't believe it. I was just bathing.'
'And at midnight, Sandy?'
'What for no? It's a guid thing bathing, at all hours.'
'And with your clothes on, Sandy?'
'What for no? I have na' always just the time to tak' aff ma' claes when I want to bathe.'

*

Tuesday, August 12
We take our long journey leisurely, and by the time we have crossed the summit [of North Glen Sannox] and begin the descent towards Chalmadale the hot, blue noon is over us. It is really hot—one of the few days of the year of which this could be said, and we make a protracted halt at what is called the Witches' Bridge. I have not been able to find any legend attached to the locality, but I suppose it must be a place where some berated shepherd, hurrying down from the dark moorland, fancied that the witches in pursuit of him were cut off, as in 'Tam o'Shanter', by the running water. It looks no place for a cold, northern witch or fiend now—rather a haunt for the happy naiad and the gamesome faun.

The stream at this bridge comes down a little scaur in the hillside. The water is clear and sparkling, and the banks are covered with soft cushions of moss and heather; so here we dispose ourselves in half a dozen groups. One of our young swains makes music on his pipe; my friend John More murmurs appropriate lines from the Choric song in the 'Lotus Eaters', about hearing the downward stream with half-shut eyes. Then it is proposed that we should make nonsense-verses, and the Reckless Rhymester, lying on his back and watching the smoke curl from his cigarette, finishes that amusement with the following tune:

> Sing you a song of Loch Ranza,
> And knock it all off in a stanza;
>> There's a castle, the mountains, a bay,
>> And an inn, where they frizzle all day
> Enough for the paunch of a Panza,
>> The herrings they catch in the bay
>> At Loch Ranza.
>
> *

Friday, August 15

...we come upon a sedate and yet happy company of peasants and fisher-folk from the village [of Corrie]. Their demeanour is in accord with the landscape. We pause and talk with them. They have been to some little week-night meeting for devotion held at the manse, and the young man who is their pastor is setting them forward on their way home. It is pleasant to listen to their talk—gossip without garrulousness or levity, the quiet and simple interchange of news about what interests them in the cottage and on the sea. Most of them are elderly women, but there are also some men and boys. Among them is poor Janet McBride. She is lame; but they walk slowly enough even for her. Janet is a 'lone woman'—she has neither chick nor child, and lives in a queer little cabin of wood in which there is only just room for a fire and a couch. She came to the island as a servant when she was but a girl, and has lived on it ever since, and they will not send her away. She spins wool on an old wheel and knits a few stockings; but her fingers are stiff with rheumatism, and if those who are themselves poor enough were not kind to her it would go ill with Janet in the winter-time. When we reached the lane which turns from the high road by the sea and runs up into South Sannox Glen, we bade good-night to Janet and her friends. Their faces showed how happy they were, and I said to my companion, 'Who would rob them of that which not only breaks the monotony of their existence, but which also brings to them consolation of the highest kind?'

*

Tuesday, August 26

At Corrie there are no yachts. Of this we have little right to complain: even in Eden there were omissions. At the same time we had set our minds upon having at least one short cruise under canvas; and, after many protracted sessions, the boys carried a resolution in favour of our hiring for a day the best and trimmest trading-smack that we could find. We fixed on the *Blue Bell* because she was the handsomest and cleanest-looking craft; and then we confided our intentions to Willie McNiven, the younger brother of the owner. Willie is the model boatman of Corrie; so much of a model that sometimes we can't help laughing at his obvious, and yet unintentional, resemblance to the Jack-tar of the stage. He is splendidly built, muscular, and lithe; his head is thickly set with black curling hair, and his face is both handsome in form and open in expression. It would not be much of an exaggeration to say that he wears a perennial smile; the difficulty, indeed, is to catch him when he is not smiling. If you do succeed in coming upon him at a time when he is so far off his guard, the lapse is only momentary. Upon the slightest provocation the smile comes back and spreads over his features, as the sunshine spreads over a green field in April when the light clouds are flying across the sky. He would make his fortune among the London studios, and Poynter or Leighton would find him as useful as Hook. In short, his whole personality is a thing to admire and rejoice in.

George Milner *Studies of Nature on the Coast of Arran* (London: Longmans, Green, and Co., 1894)

Sheep-Shearing in Arran
George Eyre-Todd, 1895

There is a certain green hollow among the Arran hills, where every summer the typical scene of Highland pastoral life is repeated in all details as it has occurred probably for a century past. Seven or eight hundred sheep, perhaps, are to be shorn, and it is a time of neighbourly help and hearty good cheer, the rivalry of ambitious shearers, and the airing of quaint hill wit.

For days the shepherd has been working his scattered flocks lower and lower among the mountains. In a deep burn-pool at the bottom of a secluded glen between the hills there has been a great washing of the herds—a mighty plunging and splashing in the swirling torrent, and emergence of snowy fleeces. In the fields about the shieling all the short summer night before the event, there has been a multitudinous bleating and movement of the flocks, followed about sunrise perhaps, by a pursuit of miles after some escaping ewe. The shepherd, who has been up before daybreak casting anxious glances at the weather, and once more counting his charge, has been joined early in the morning by some of his nearest neighbours among the hills, and has already been busy for hours separating sheep and lambs, and getting the former, duly assorted, in readiness into the folds.

Glen Rosa

Great preparations likewise have been made indoors by the shepherd's wife. Huge bunches of vegetables have been cleaned, chopped up, and placed in the boiler, to be made, with the joints sent up from 'the big hoose', into mutton broth; a large boxful of scones and oatmeal cakes has been baked, the flat iron girdle swinging for half a day over the kitchen fire; and a whole cheese has been laid in. The end of the shieling in which the fleeces are to be stored has been cleared out, the shearing trestles have been got down from their resting-place and set in a semicircle on the green before the door, and in the midst of them a fire has been kindled, and a pot of Archangel tar set on it to boil. There is great glee among the shepherd's children, who get a holiday from school to help on the occasion. With bare brown legs they run everywhere, laughing, the work of their elders being play to them; and the eldest daughter, a blowing rose of some eighteen summers, has put a bit of fresh ribbon round her modest throat, and as she goes about helping her mother, has a heightened colour on her cheek. It might be cruel to ask the reason why.

Along the moorland paths, presently the shepherds who are to lend their help can be seen coming in, each with his long hazel staff in hand and a collie or two at his heels. Weather-beaten men of middle age, most of these Highland shepherds are, with heavy blue bonnets, hob-nailed shoes, and rough homespun tweeds, their faces hidden behind prodigious bushy beards. Only one or two are young, clean-shaven all but a short whisker, and, from the sly chaffing which they are made to undergo, apparently still bachelors.

'Weel, Angus, I'm thinkin' ye ken this road better than maist of us. Was't a lost yowe ye were after up here on Tuesday nicht, or was't a pair o' blue een?'

'Mind, Angus, it's to be shearin' sheep ye're here the day, an' no to be castin' sheep's een at Janet MacIntyre.'

Under banter of this sort, sometimes Angus would be the better of a little more hair on his face to hide his confusion. Nor is he greatly consoled on reaching the shieling, for Janet somehow just then, of course, is nowhere to be seen. It is only a little later that she will happen in on some chance errand, perhaps when Angus is alone packing fleeces in the byre-end of the house.

For awhile there is nothing but a succession of greetings in English and Gaelic. '*Deimir a tha thuan diugh?*' '*Tha gu maith.*' 'And how is the wife an' the bairns, John? An' is the wee laddie better that had the fever?' The collies effect their own doubtful reconnaissances in dog fashion, walking round each other with suspicious sniffs and jealous growls, finally quieted by an anathema from their masters, or the thump of a stone on the ribs.

Then the work of the day begins. The sheep are caught in the folds and carried to the trestles, their legs tied if they prove restive. As a rule, they lie on their backs peacefully enough, being quite helpless in that position. Each man has brought his own pair of clipping-shears, a strong instrument of broad blades and sharp points, with a steel spring, which recoils open in the hand. Sitting astride the narrow end of the trestle, he holds the sheep with his left hand, and cuts close to the skin with his right, stripping the matted fleece off the animal in one broad unbroken sheet. There is great rivalry, of course, in the matter of clipping, and it is amazing with what speed and neatness most of the men get through their work. Notwithstanding that the wool is clipped close to the skin, hardly ever is a drop of blood drawn, and in these rare cases a touch of the tar-stick makes all right. When the work is fairly set going, the shepherd himself and an assistant are kept busy, catching the sheep, examining them, and bringing them up to the trestles. A bit clipped out of the ear, sometimes a brand on the hoof, marks the ownership. This has to be looked to. Sometimes the end of a horn which threatens hurt has to be sawn off; and other little matters get attention. As each sheep is clipped and springs to its feet, the shepherd's boy, delighted with the occupation, stands ready with the owner's stamp, and, dipping it in the tar-pot, claps it to the animal's side. Then the poor beast is let go, and, lightened of its covering, takes to the hill, bewildered, an utter stranger for awhile even to its own lamb. Not a little touching is it to see the lamb; run out from the flock at its mother's accustomed call, only to start back, unrecognising, from the thin white ghost that comes to meet it. And all day long, as the sheep are let go, the hillside echoes with the piteous bleatings.

All day long, too, bits of light chaff and quaintly turned hill gossip pass from mouth to mouth among the shearers, though hands and eyes are fully occupied; and when dinner-time comes, about twelve o' clock, and the steaming broth and mutton are brought out, it is Janet's turn to stand a little sly banter.

96

'I wad gie a croun, Janet, to ken wha gied ye that bit o' red ribbon at the fair.'

'Never heed helpin' Angus there to mair broth, lassie. He does a' his feastin' wi' his een when he comes up here.'

Janet, nevertheless, sometimes gives as good as she gets, in spite of her blushes; and many a hearty laugh rings out when her shafts hit home. For the oldest married man on the ground is himself something more than half in love with the blithe, bonnie lass.

And so the day wears on under the sunny blue sky; and, at night, when the last sheep is off the trestles, there is steaming black tea in readiness, with abundance of scones and oatcakes and cheese to be disposed of, and, perhaps, to finish with, and to keep out the cold evening air of the moors, a *deoch an dorus* from the black bottle, as the neighbourly helpers separate to take their way homeward among the glens.

George Eyre-Todd (1862-1937) *Vignettes of the North* (Glasgow: Morison Brothers, 1895)

Fairy Stories
Alexander Carmichael, 1895

Gruagach, a supernatural female who presided over cattle and took a kindly interest in all that pertained to them. In return a libation of milk was made to her when the women milked the cows in the evening. If the oblation were neglected, the cattle, notwithstanding all precautions, were found broken loose and in the corn; and if still omitted, the best cow in the fold was found dead in the morning. The offering was poured on 'clach na gruagaich', the 'gruagach' stone.

*

Each district gives its own local colouring to the 'gruagach'. The following account was given to me by a woman at West Bennan in Arran in August 1895:—

The 'gruagach' lived at East Bean in a cave which is still called 'uamh na gruagaich'—cave of the 'gruagach', and 'uamh na beiste'—cave of the monster. She herded the cattle of the townland of Bennan, and no spring-loss, no death-loss, no mishap, no murrain, ever befell them, while they throve and fattened and multiplied right well.

The 'gruagach' would come forth with the radiant sun, her golden hair streaming on the morning breeze, and her rich voice filling the air with melody. She would wait on a grassy hillock afar off till the people would bring out their 'creatairean', creatures, crooning a lullaby the while, and striding to and fro. The following is a fragment of one of her songs:—

> Ho, hi, ho! mach na boidhean,
> Boidhean boidheach brogach beennach,
> Ho, hi, ho! mach na boidhean.

> Crodh Mhicugain, crodh Mhiceannain,
> Crodh MhicFhearachair mhoir a Bheannain,
> Ho, hi, ho! mach na boidhean.

> Corp us carn air graisg na Beurla,
> Mharbh iad orm mo cheile falaich,
> Ho, hi, ho! mach na boidhean.

> Ruisg iad mi gu ruig mo leine,
> Struill agus streuill mo leannan,
> Ho, hi, ho! mach na boidhean.

> Oidhch an Arainn, oidhch an Ile,
> 'S an Cinntire uaine a bharraich,
> Ho, hi, ho! mach na boidhean.

> Ho, hi, ho! out the kine,
> Pretty cattle hoofed and horned,
> Ho, hi, ho! out the kine.

> Cows of Macugan, Cows of Mackinnon,
> Cows of the big Macfarquar of the Bennan,
> Ho, hi, ho! out the kine.

> Corpse and cairn to the rabble English,
> They have killed my hidden lover,
> Ho, hi, ho! out the kine.

> They have stripped me to my shift,
> They have clubbed and torn my lover,
> Ho, hi, ho! out the kine.

> A night in Arran, a night in Isaly,
> And in green Kintyre of birches,
> Ho, hi, ho! out the kine.

The people of Bennan were so pleased with the tender care the 'gruagach' took of their corn and cattle that they resolved to give her a linen garment to clothe her body and down sandals to cover her feet. They placed these on a knoll near the 'gruagach' and watched from afar. But instead of being grateful she was offended, and resented their intrusion so much that she determined to leave the district. She placed her left foot on Ben Bhuidhe in Arran and her right foot on 'Allasan', Ailsa Craig, making this her stepping-stone to cross to the mainland of Scotland or to Ireland. While the 'gruagach' was in the act of moving her left foot, a three-masted ship passed beneath, the mainmast of which struck her in the thigh and overturned her into the sea. The people of Bennan mourned the 'gruagach' long and loudly, and bewailed their own officiousness.

*

Donald MacAlastair, aged seventy-nine, crofter, Druim-a-ghinnir, Arran, told me the following story on the 28th of August 1895:—

'Bha na sifri a fuireach 's an tom agus bha nabuidh aca agus bhiodh an duine dol air cheilidh do thaigh nan sifri. Bha an duine a gabhail beachd air doigh nan sifri agus a deanamh mar bhiodh iad a deanamh.

'Thog na sifri turas orra gu dol a dh'Eirinn, agus thog an duine air gu falbh leo. Rug a chuile sifri riamh air geo-astair, agus chaidh e casa-gobhlach air a gheo-astair, agus a nunn cuan na h-Eire bha iad muin air mhuin a chuile glun diubh ann an tiota, agus a nunn cuan na h-Eire bha an duine as an deoghaidh casagobhlach air geo-astair mar aon do chacha. Dh'eubh sifri beag biteach, bronach, an robh iad uile deas agus dh'eubh cacha uile gu'n robh, agus dh'eubh an sifri beag—

> 'Mo righ air mo cheann,
> Dol thairis am dheann,
> Air chirean nan tonn,
> A dh' Eirinn.'

'Lean mise,' orsa righ nan sifrean, agus a mach a bha iad nunn air muir a chuile mac mathar dhiubh casa-gobhlach air a gheo-astair. Cha robh fios aig MacCuga air thalamh ciamar a thilleadh e a thir a mhuinntiris a rithist ach leum e air a gheo-astair mar a chunnaic e na sifrean a deanamh, agus dh'eubh e mar a chuala e iadsan a g'eubhach agus ann an tiota bha e air ais ann an Arainn. Ach fhuair e a leor dhe na sifrich an turas sin fhein, agus cha d'fhalbh e riamh tuilleadh leo.'

'The fairies were dwelling in the knoll, and they had a near neighbour who was wont to visit them in their home. The man used to observe the ways of the fairies and to do as they did.

'The fairies took a journey upon them to go to Ireland, and the man took upon him to go with them. Every single fairy caught a ragwort and went astride the ragwort, and they were pell-mell, every knee of them, across the Irish ocean in an instant, and across the Irish ocean was the man after them, astride a ragwort like one of the others. A little wee tiny fairy shouted and asked were they all ready, and all the others replied that they were, and the little fairy called out—

99

'My king at my head,
Going across in my haste,
On the crests of the waves,
To Ireland.'

'Follow me,' said the king of the fairies, and away they were across the Irish ocean, each mother's son of them astride his ragwort. Macuga (Cook) did not know on earth how he would return to his native land, but he leapt upon the ragwort as he saw the fairies do, and he called as he heard them call, and in an instant he was back in Arran. But he had got enough of the fairies on this trip itself, and he never went with them again.'

Alexander Carmichael ed. *Carmina Gadelica* vol. II (Edinburgh and London: Oliver and Boyd, 1928)

Hamish at the Glen
Stazel Dene, 1898

The days passed only too swiftly and after all, Hamish had had a jolly good time of it. They spent a day in doing 'the saddle' and 'Glen Sannox', and crowned it with a splendid tea at Mrs Martin's. They made again, the ascent of Goatfell, towards midnight, in the expectation of seeing the sunrise, and were rewarded with a glorious view. Tired and hungry, they were thankful to be home in time for an early breakfast at the Glen. But the night before Hamish left, was the best of all. Out in the beautiful Bay with its waters like a millpond, they listened to the music from the yachts which had put in for their final cruise. The bright sails glistened in the sun, setting behind Bhen Nuis while in the East the moon was rising above the Ayrshire Coast, and the shadows of Goatfell and the Castle Woods sank deep into the Bay. The Gortchen and Hamish were accompanied in their boat by two of Arran's beauties and what more could be desired—the maidens cheered the youths, with their sweet voices, singing,

'In the gloaming, O my darling,
When the lights are dim and low
And the shadows swiftly falling
Softly come and softly go.'

but adieu fair Isle.

Stazel Dene *The Gortchen: A Tale of an Arran Glen* (London: Digby, Long & Co., 1898)

The Heliotrope Bretelles

'Hari-Kari' (Robert Browning), 1910

In Glasgow town there's wondrous store
　　Of summering finerie,
But nothing so neat as Maisie wore,
　　At the head of Lochranza quay.
Yet it wasn't her blouse's graceful cut
　　That snared me with its spells,
Nor the dainty lace of the collar—but
　　The heliotrope Bretelles.

O! all the summer long, I've been
　　In many a pleasant place,
And many a muslin blouse I've seen
　　With a collar of Valence lace;
And many no doubt were nice and neat,
　　And were worn by charming belles;
But they needed one thing to be quite complete—
　　The heliotrope Bretelles.

And if ever I have the luck to get
　　Another such holiday,
My wandering sail once more I'll set
　　Across Lochranza Bay.
And there I shall sally around the house
　　In a jacket with long lapels,
And Maisie will wear her muslin blouse
　　With the heliotrope Bretelles.

Hari-Kari (Robert Browning) *Songs of Two Cities* (Glasgow & Dalbeattie, 1910)

A Strange Story

T.C.F. Brotchie, 1911

It may be recalled that within the old grey keep of Kildonan the last Barclay, Baron of Ardrossan, known as the 'De'il of Ardrossan', ended his wretched days. He it was who set his Satanic Majesty to erect a bridge from Cumbrae to the mainland, but as it was approaching completion some luckless stranger happening to mention the Divinity, immediately Satan vanished in a flame of fire, overwhelming the bridge, but leaving the foundations, which may be seen to this day, one on the Cumbrae and the other near West Kilbride. Barclay retired afterwards to Kildonan. He had a presentiment that should he ever set foot on Irish ground he should no longer live. The legend had it that one day some Irish fishing boats put into Kildonan cove. They brought with them some sods which they left on the beach. Barclay, chancing as he passed to tread on them, inquired how they came there. Being told, he exclaimed that his end was now come, and giving orders regarding the disposal of his corpse, he is said to have died that very night. He commanded that his body should be sewn in a bull's hide and buried within sea mark on the shore beneath Kildonan Peel. This was punctually attended to, but the legend tells us the sea washed off the sand, and the body floated across the Firth to Ardrossan, where it was taken up and finally found a resting-place in the old chapel.

T.C.F. Brotchie *Scottish Western Holiday Haunts* (Glasgow and Edinburgh: John Menzies, 1911)

Wild Monamore

William Brown, 1912

There's beauty around me, there's beauty above,
The Ross and the Urie—like me and my love—
Entwined by a brooklet that sings to the sea;
But love is the stream 'tween my lassie and me.

The heather blooms fresh on the sloping hillside,
The branches hang green where the cool waters glide
O'er rock and o'er pebbles, delightsome and free,
Like the love that flows on 'tween my lassie and me.

Ferns grow for my lover, all mossy and green,
There's music, wild flowers, and a cosy leaf screen;
Red deer kiss the streamlet, birds sing as they soar
O'er the dark, shaded waters of wild Monamore.

O, sweet is the sound of thy swift-flowing rill,
And soft are the bleatings hill echoes to hill,
Thy beauties, enchanting and grand tho' they be,
Are nought to the charms of my lassie to me.

William Brown *Gleniffer and Glen Rosa and other poems* (Paisley: Alexander Gardner, 1912)

Lochranza (photograph by J. Valentine)

The Arran Smacks
(These useful little craft are now getting out-of-date.)
Paddy Coffey, c.1920

Shon McPhail was an Arran man,
    And a mariner bold was he;
He owned a smack called the Betsy Ann,
    Which he sailed through the briny sea.

He lifted his sand in Lamlash Bay,
    And rockery stones as well;
Then for Glasgow city he sailed away,
    The stones and his sand to sell.

Tatties and scadans, some bread and kail
    Were the stores that he had on board;
For the times were bad, and Shon McPhail
    Could no better than these afford.

'Heigh, ho!' he says, 'it's gey hard on me
    That, after a fortnight's run,
I maun sell my sand on the Glesca Quay
    At five or six bob a ton.

Then load up coals for hame again
    At a most ridiculous freight,
And their reason for this, they tell me plain,
    Is because I'm no' up-to-date.'

The puffers, he says, have killed his trade,
    And the days of the smacks have gone;
And there isn't a living now to be made
    For the likes of poor old Shon.

Though things for him look mighty black,
    Still it never can be denied,
It was men like him and his Arran smack
    That helped to make the Clyde.

Paddy Coffey *Pickings from the Poetical Works* (Edinburgh & Glasgow: John Menzies, [c.1920])

Isle of Arran: Grandeur on Glasgow's Doorstep
Neil Munro, 1923

About thirty years ago, the writer of an article on Arran in one of the English weekly reviews fervently thanked Heaven that the Duke of Hamilton had kept his isle 'unspoiled'. By this the writer meant the preservation of a solitary privacy agreeable to his own mood during a week or two of summer holidays. He found the ducal policy of no feuing, no fixity of tenure, no dogs, and a severe discouragement of summer lodgers thoroughly to his taste; probably he had a memory of refined exclusiveness as a guest in Duchery Lodge and the deer forests.

But Arran was not specially set apart by the Almighty in the estuary of the Clyde to be for ever a pleasure ground for a handful of privileged people in a brief season of escape from the crowded and bustling urban lives they are content to live most parts of the year. Sooner or later the old feudal fences were bound to be broken down by the sheer involuntary thrust of two million people in the immediate neighbourhood outside. So Arran is not what it was when *The Saturday Review* piously held it up to our admiration as a justification of the grand old autocratic landlordism.

There is fixity of tenure now in Arran, feus are granted almost everywhere. If you want storm-windows, a certain height of roof, baths and other sanitary amenities in your house, you can have them. There is even a public hospital at Lamlash (by public subscription), and some day there is almost certain to be a secondary school, and a West-side harbour.

Arran, in short, is being what the writer of thirty years ago would regard as vulgarised. Rare poetic souls (at a distance), will be horrified to learn it has now the telephone and that the Tin Lizzies of quite inconspicuous natives dash numerously and impetuously over the String Road, which, you remember, you used to walk with grandpa painfully to Shiskin.

An annual journalistic joke of the Spring-time used to be 'The cuckoo was heard on Saturday in Arran for the first time this year, by the kind permission of the Duke of Hamilton.' On wireless sets now, Arran can hear band-programmes in the cities, and all the Dukes in Christendom can't prevent them. There may, for all I know, be pierrots at Lamlash and occasional 'movies' at Blackwaterfoot, though I think not. Yet Lamlash and Brodick, Corrie and Kildonan, and all that East side of Arran which has inspired the charming stories of Mr A. Boyd Scott, are still more 'foreign' and natural than the shores of Cowal and the bays of Bute and Ayrshire.

One hears old-timers who remember Arran in the days when natives took in the hens' meat because of passing Glasgow folk, lamenting some

Fullarton's cart

105

vague rural qualities missing now in its atmosphere. What they really miss is their own youth, when leaky skylights were a joy, short beds a great experience, and the sea was good enough to bath in, and something of romance was in all primitive discomforts.

Arran can't be 'spoiled'; it is much too intractable a whim of nature. Its ports and villages usurp but trivial little areas of old raised sea-beach; in the mass it remains as wild and solitary as when Bruce and Fingal hunted in its forests. I have spoken of two million people in its immediate propinquity; only the merest fraction of them know anything at all of Arran, though it is accessible in two hours from St. Enoch Station; the fascinations of the sophisticated Isle of Man are more to their taste than the glens and mountains.

I know a Glasgow man who, at the age of sixty, never was in Arran till some weeks ago, though almost every other island of the West of Scotland was familiar to him. He was astonished and chagrined to have left the Isle of Arran so long unvisited.

'Blind ignorance!' he confessed to me in explanation. 'I had seen no more of Arran close at hand than can be compassed in a call of the Campbeltown steamer at Lochranza quay. I somehow got the impression that it wasn't my kind of country, for I'm of the kind who better love to hear the whaup scream than the mouse cheep. Its name got spoiled for me by seeing it too much on Broomielaw shipping-boxes, and I could not believe a place so close to Glasgow was not trampled down by the feet of the Glasgow Fair.

'But there were other things that influenced me to keep me away from Arran—the most potent, I fancy, that cynical retaliative tradition of the Glasgow people for whom so long its owners never had a welcome. All Glasgow's Arran stories were about the island's unattractive features—poor houses and factorial prohibitions the worst of them. How was I to know that I was foolishly turning my back on 165 square miles of the grandest scenery in Europe?'

Yet ten minutes' intelligent preoccupation with a map could have removed my friend's misapprehensions. It will take him all the rest of his life to get acquainted with Arran, and even then he shall not have exhausted half its charms. Poor soul! he has not seen the winter sunrise light up all those little eastern towns and hamlets from Corrie, under Cioch na 'h-oighe, to Kildonan. He has all that western shore from the Cock to Sliddery to learn at different seasons, but alas! he is much too late to extract the ultimate pang of pleasure from dunes and sands of Machrie, sea-holly's bloom, and swimming in the surf of Kilbrannan Sound.

And then the glens and bens! There are no more impressive features of the kind in Britain. Their very names inspire and tempt to wandering—Glen Chalmadale, Glen Sannox, Glen Sheraig, Glen Iorsa, Glen Rosa, and Glen Cloy. Few of them, from old, were probably more than sparsely tenanted, but Chalmadale, that exquisite little valley between Corrie and

Lochranza, was once the most populous in Arran. It is less than a hundred years since 500 of its people emigrated en masse to Chaleur Bay, New Brunswick; their abandoned hearths are visible still among the nettles.

As for mountains—look from the mainland when the sun is setting, or come suddenly upon them, lifting through the mist, on the rise, 'twixt Brodick and Lamlash, and speculate on what weeks of climbing, what seasons of incomplete familiarity they give scope for.

Arran is, in its way, an epitome of all Scotland save Scotland's uglier features. There is even a hint of England in the wide expanses of the Shiskin Valley. Cliffs, caves, and sandy creeks round all its shores make it a most ideal haunt for youth; its resident novelist, Mr Sillars, has to himself a territory far more inspirational and romantic than Hall Caine had in the Isle of Man.

'Neither is there,' in the word of old William Lithgow, written three hundred years ago, 'any isle like to it for brave gentry and hill-hovering hunters.'

Neil Munro (1863-1930) *Glasgow Evening News* 24 September 1923

The Bonny Lads o' Corrie
'R.M. Featherpick', 1923

Four gallant lads sat i' the Inn
Drinking the bluid red wine:
'Oh whaur shall we walk this day in three
On this Isle we've lo'ed lang syne?'

Then up and spak the Sheriff bold,
A guidly lad was he—
'Oh I'm for roond the Fallen Rocks—
Will ony come wi' me?'

Laith, laith were the ither three
To weet their Phillips shoon,
In the crossing o' the Sannox Burn,
Whaur the merry fish come doon.

But Charlie K.'s the best climber
That ever clamb the scree,
An' he wad up the high Goatfell
In steps but barely three.

Sir Wattie he spak a wisely word:
'An what for wad ye sweit?
Gie me my pipe, gie me my book
An' I'll snooze at the water's meet.'

But t'ither Charles, he ruled them a'
Wi' a word, but barely three,
'We'll find the heid o' the Sannox Glen,
An' ye'll a' maun follow me.'

They hadna gaen a step, a step,
A step but barely ane,
When up there sprang twa heather coos
And the Sheriff sat doon on a stane.

Half o'er, half o'er tae Keer Vawr
They found a bieldy nuik,
And there they laid wee Wattie doon
Wi' his pipe, his snooze, his buik.

Oh! laith, laith were the Charlies twa
Tae lay them doon sae sune,
And lang ere mony an hour had gane
They'd reached the hills abune.

Half o'er, half o'er the Keer Vawr
Wee Charles dropped oot o' the race,
But Charles the strang wi' steppis lang
Sune reached the summit's face.

And sune he stood on the saddle top,
And mony a thocht gied he
To the three bonny Scots lairds in Sannox Glen
Lyin' wearyin' for their tea.

Oh lang lang did the lairdis sit
As they smoked their pipes alane,
But lang ere the red sun had set
They'd a' gane home again.

An' ev'ry May that comes his roon'
In Bonny Scotland's year
Shall see these four braw bonny lads
Drink deep of Corrie's cheer.

'R. M. Featherpick' from *Arran in Spring (1879-1937)* edited by Charles Ker (London and Glasgow: Blackie, 1937)

Common Things Like Stick Gathering, Tinker Folk and House-Cleaning

John Sillars, 1925

Even in the very worst times in Park, ay, in the dead of winter, there would be nights of laughter. In these days if peats were wet and the back-end of the year stormy, it was no uncommon thing for folks to be without coals for weeks. And in these days it was death by the law to lift firewood from the plantings. Rotten branches, fallen trees, all these belonged to the Duke (so his foresters said), and yet children must have a fire coming home from school, wringing wet, as like as not, and with little bellies craving food like young wolves; the mid-day 'piece', oatcake and cheese, scone and butter, or dripping, or scone and bramble jelly, was long forgotten by four o'clock, and the morning plate of porridge and milk ages away. On such a time, with the smack storm-bound for weeks, the smell of burning wood pervaded the village of Park, and this is how the burning wood was obtained.

Anne McMillan would put a shawl about her head and shoulders and take a walk along to see Biddy, and you may be sure Mrs Currie would join her with a shawl round her shoulders likewise, and they would be no sooner in Biddy's kitchen when the door would open and Mrs Cragg would come in.

'Are your coals finished, Biddy?' Anne would ask. And Biddy would point to the fire—'Oh, sorrow a cruttle have I.' And a smile would come about her lips and eyes as she saw the devilment rise in Anne's face.

'Well, we'll go and gather a bundle of sticks.' Anne would get hold of one of the children then, and start to strip him. 'Put you the weans to bed, Biddy—come you here, Donald,' for there was a third son growing now, and promising to outstrip Guy and James. And Donald would suffer Anne to strip him and wash his feet and legs, for as sure as fate, she would have some kind of sweetie for him. And when the boys were in bed, the lamp would be screwed down until such times as they would sleep. And Anne had as many tricks to go through with Donald first, for he was a serious child—a kind of natural minister. Anne would stand up, a great strapping girl, and raise her hand above her head. 'God bless all in this house, Donald,' she would say, and the boy would put up his arm in imitation and repeat the lesson, and Biddy would tell Anne to give over—'for the child frightens me,' she would say.

And as sure as the wick was turned low, Anne would have some devilish tale to recount; maybe it would be foreign sailors ashore and prowling, or a daft man loose somewhere, for there were many strangers boarded out on lonely farms here and there, usually dipsomaniacs who at the beginning of every month appeared well-dressed and flush of money, and at the end thereof, wild-eyed and given to night raking. These tales were for the benefit of Mrs Currie, who was a Glasgow woman and sat in sheer terror, being afraid to go home alone, and more afraid to go stick gathering. Biddy said of her, 'She is the nicest soul that ever drew breath, and always busy, always in a guddle, always wearying for the trim houses and streets of Glasgow, and it is always her washing day whenever her man comes home.' And as for Mrs Cragg, she was a born story-teller with the finest memory that was ever heard tell of, and I think her stories were mostly old folk tales, for they never varied a word in the telling. As Biddy said, 'When Anne got rid of her most prodigious lie, off went Mrs Cragg on some dread and eerie tale—told in whispers and with the greatest skill, in the dim glow from the lamp, until poor Mrs Currie was trembling with fear, and that was Anne's delight. Out she would go then, and Biddy holding on to her, for Anne knew every path and the slaps in every hedge off by heart, as the children say. And it seemed as if the very devil himself was let loose in her on these ploys. She would stop suddenly and whisper, 'What's that—did you hear it?' till Mrs Currie was like to drop with fear. Whatever tale Anne told inside, be sure that that tale was utilised in the darkness of the wood, and she thought no more of laughing in the dead of night, with the Lord knows what near her, than she did in the lighted room. She would pull Biddy like mad until they had out-distanced the poor Glasgow woman, and then wait listening. 'Wait till you hear her, Biddy,' she would say, 'the frightened little devil.' And sure enough Mrs Currie's voice would come wailing, 'Oh, wait for me, you heartless creature.' And at that Anne would laugh as heartily as a sailor.

Each woman made up her bundle, a back-burden of dry faggots with the crotal growing on them, it's likely, and stooped beneath the weight of their load, they made their way home, and hid their sticks beneath a kitchen bed, or somewhere out of sight. You may be sure there would be a cup of tea in the small hours till Mrs Currie would gather herself together, and in the morning the porridge pot would be sottering on the fire with the meal bursting into little volcanoes.

Away there the tinkers, travelling the country and routed from the village, assumed a great boldness, nor did they refrain from kicking at a locked door or hammering on a window. But it would be stranger tinkers that would do the like of that, for the real tinkers were as well known to the children as the shepherds' dogs. There was the umbrella man who had been a soldier, and was most desperately wicked-looking with a black patch over his eye, and Old White Head, who sold bone combs and whangs—whangs were rare leather boot-laces that would last a year easy. John Bell sold bottles of blue, and was a great performer on the melodeon, playing the cantiest little tunes you ever listened to. These, and a host of others who travelled the country with bowls and dishes, were household words in Park.

When the spring came—and how Biddy and the children wearied for spring—the spring work was commenced. Alick and Neil would have the garden delved, but that was the least of it. There was the wrack for the potatoes to be cut from the rocks, if the sea did not throw it up all ready for lifting on the shore-head. You would see Mrs Currie there and Mrs Cragg, and the McMillans' cart and the McKelvies' carts and the Crawfords' cart, all thrang at the wrack gathering, and many a woman's eye looked longingly at the carts that were so easily filled as she trailed with a back-burden of wet tangle on her back from the shore to her garden a mile away. But to hear Biddy you would think it was child's play.

She would wave her hand at a catkin tree in bloom, and her children had no need to hear words for the delight in her voice; she would show them a bank starred with primroses, and 'Don't pull them, dears,' she would say, 'they're happier out here than in a glass of water.' I think that never did she so much as raise her voice to her children in anger, and yet from the oldest to the youngest, they would run to do her pleasure. There would be a great day splitting seed—cutting up potatoes into as many pieces as they had eyes or growths. The wrack was put into the drills and the seeds planted, and the Lord saw that they grew. And there was great competition at the gardening, especially at the weeding time, every one striving to outrise every one else, and have so many drills weeded before their neighbours were on the ground. The cottar women would be out in McKelvie's field giving a day to old John at the planting, and he would have a word for every one. 'Man, it does my heart good to see folk that can work. We could show them how to work on the other side.' And then, God bless you, the garden would be no sooner planted and the spring work under way, than the house-cleaning was started. Everything was scoured to the last pot lid, and as sure as the spring came round Mrs Currie took lumbago and went about her work 'two double', as Anne McMillan said.

These, Biddy said, were her happiest days. With the spring the old paper was stripped from the walls—walls that were discoloured with rain-water from a leak in the roof, and grew strange hairy-looking moulds like those in the inside of a jam-pot newly opened. Then there was the new paper to choose, and neighbours in studying the paper-book and doubling back the trysted patterns; there were days when the kitchen was coiled round with the selvedge edge of the new papers, and the paste-brush schlaried everybody who came near. The blankets were scoured, with what a tramping of feet, and laid out on hedges until all the hedgerows round every house had their woolly burden. There was a lick of paint for the windows, and heaven knows what black-leading and black-lacquering went on at the fireplaces. Carpets were beat and mats battered unmercifully, stripped bedtick beds bulged from every window, and clean fresh gravel was scattered before the doors. What washing and what ironing and starching, and what praise each woman body had for the other—a new piece of waxcloth before a chest of drawers was a triumph of art—(and a little more on the rent)—and how clean the houses looked with the picture-frames polished and everything shining— the window curtains all fluffed out and tied with ribbon and fairly cracking with the pride and stiffness of them. The sun would be over the hills at last and shining on new red earth. The big houses would be let for the season, or maybe for the two middle months or with a change of tenant for August and September, but mostly the little houses were let for each month separately. And the visitors would be in delight over the cleanness and cosiness of the rooms before the native women, who had a knack of being ladylike, and probably in secret laughed themselves silly, pondering where to stow their clothes, because in these out-of-the-way places, although rich folk can wear anything, they usually produce only their very finest costumes and skirts and blouses to make the rustics stare— possibly on a Sabbath.

Biddy dearly loved the field work, laughing at the language of Anne, who never failed to find someone worthy of a good swearing, if it were young John for driving the horses too hard, or the old man sitting watching the young babies. And Mrs Cragg, who took great pleasure in little nippy remarks how so-and-so's stern was like a Dutch smack, or 'look at that one running about to show young John her cleverness,' was worth her place too. She was so clever always to find out the hidden purpose, and had always every little tittle-tattle of news from far and near to whisper, as a dead secret.

And every cottar would have a drill or maybe two drills of potatoes in the field of their very own, and mind you, these were the carefully tended drills, all except Mrs Cragg's, for hers were never covered properly to her mind. 'It's weel seen I'm not a favourite, like some folks,' she would say— 'look at him slashing on the horses to spoil my drill.'

*

There were great days at the change of the months—great yoking of horses—double machines and waggonettes to drive the gentry to the steamer—great carting of trunks and baskets, hampers, and leather cases— goodly tips to be slipped into waistcoat pockets against a future dearth of coins, and all the buzz of preparing for the new folk, oh, very nice genteel families. The folk would be scarcely settled and all together when the men would be cutting the roads round the harvest-fields, and that was the time of times for work. There was no 'wha lies there?' these mornings, when the scythes were swishing through the grain. It was then a body must show their suppleness—it was then that neighbours must help, or weans go without meal somewhere.

*

With the gentry away back to the town to 'save up enough to come back next year', for there is a strong belief that gentry retire like rodents to holes and corners of industry during the winter and save their hard-earned pay to pay for a month's holiday at the coast.

Well, with the gentry away and the potatoes gathered, the nights began to creep in, and the jollifications began.

There would be kirns here and there, dancing and feasting in the cleared barns, and the jokes would begin before the music. The best fiddler in these parts lived on the Fiddler's ridge, and you may be sure he was in great demand on these occasions. There is a fine story of this man, who, summoned post-haste to a spree, and having accordingly filled himself to concert pitch, came to the Highburn and found it in spate. What does he do but out with his bow, and laid it across the water.

'Split water,' said he, like Moses at the Red Sea, but whether the water obliged him I never heard.

Well, as I have told you at the beginning of this chapter, these were Biddy's happiest days. The children were growing about her, and Alick was often at home and ready to take her to whatever party was toward, and every one made of her, gentle and simple alike. A clever, pleasant, hard-working woman, she turned her children out well-clad for the school and paid their coal money regularly, and was a favourite with the schoolmaster, because she had given him a wink to push Guy on.

'Here's a boy to you,' she said the first day; 'you can make a kirk or a mill of him, but,' said she, 'I'm hoping it will be a kirk.' What a pleasant world it was when the boat was in harbour, for the sea was always Biddy's dread. The meal girnel was filled every back-end, and the flour barrel, and two sheep bought and killed on a table a little way from the house, with all their neighbours bleating piteously at the smell of kindred blood spilled on the ground. With the mutton cut into handy bits and salted, with green kail and turnips, and leeks and parsley in the garden, these was always plenty of soup, and not so salt as you might think if the meat be properly soaked.

To be young and strong and active, up with the daylight to the daily round, and at night, the door shut against the storm, with the children at their books round the mother's table, or maybe Guy seated at her feet and making her listen to a bit from his story—that was Biddy's life. There was her present happiness. For the future the plans were maturing. 'Once let me get the boys schooled,' said Biddy, 'and after that there was the great wide world to conquer.'

John Sillars (1887-1954) *The Desperate Battle* (Edinburgh: Blackwood, 1925)

To an Arran Piermaster (Lately Retired)

James Nicol, 1930

James of the touzled locks and stalwart frame,
Though sorely cumbered with the weight of years,
Heed thou it not! Lo! when men hear thy name,
Before their eyes a lion's head appears!
The gang-plank rests upon an Arran shore,
Touching the isle beloved of pen and brush,
And at its end thou standest, scanning o'er
The travellers descending, 'mid a hush!

Thy wide, grey eyes take toll, with welcoming gleam,
Of scholar, merchant, and their dames in line!
And note the 'usual', with a humorous beam,
The black-robed, serious holiday-divine!
'Gosh bless my soul!' In fancy I can hear
Your Arran accent, with its ringing smack,
Fall flatteringly yet heartily on each year,
'The winter's long: I'm glad to see you back!'

An Arran welcome worth the tuppence—sure!
The tuppence, James, that paid the yearly rent!
For piers don't grow upon an open moor,
And sunken piles demand their cent. per cent.!

Brodick Bay, July 1938 (photograph by Robert Walker)

To land dry-shod upon the beauteous isle
Men gladly paid who braved the ocean's shocks,
Nor counted it loss, beneath thy genial smile,
To pay returning home to change their socks!

Full many a season in its prime thou'st seen
The pleasure-seekers, eager, trooping by
To join the motor or the 'post-machine',
And scatter far and wide 'neath Arran's sky!
And thou surveyed them with thy kindly glance,
Coming and going to the here and there,
And made thy presence felt there at thy stance
As worth remembering, like the Arran air!

Others have passed we ne'er may see again,
They stamped no mould upon the plastic cells!—
But thou remain a man of thew and brain,
Alert to answer all our steamer bells!
As travellers we meet, we melt away,
Life's voyage drifts us far apart, or near,
But whilst it lasts it makes Remembrance gay
To see thee standing on thy favoured pier!

James Nicol *A Book of Arran Verse* (Ardrossan: Arthur Guthrie, 1930)

Isle of Arran
John Joy Bell, 1933

Arran's place in the open and its comparative remoteness—though it is only fourteen miles from the nearest mainland port, Ardrossan, in Ayrshire—are part of its attraction. To many of us the word 'island' spells 'romance', and ever since the advent of steam navigation the thought of a visit to Arran has suggested—to the people of the nearer West, at any rate—an adventure not to be obtained on the sheltering shores and amid the more or less suburban amenities and conventions of the Inner Firth.

Arran has never made any great effort to gain popular favour; for more than half a century it made no effort at all, offering nothing but its own rude, beautiful, unsophisticated self. Advertising pays, but so may aloofness, and Arran had all the visitors it could accommodate. No doubt the natives wished for more and bigger and better houses, but the Duke of Hamilton was not going to have his island 'spoiled'. In the nineteenth century city families accustomed to abundance in space and comfort packed themselves, willingly, blithely, into stuffy little comfortless cottages, with boxlike bedrooms and no water-supply, and for a month or two rejoiced (with, maybe, the exception of the poor mother) in what they took to be the simple life. Since then, however—the embargo on building having been removed in the nineties—there have been many changes, and the visitor is no longer expected to 'rough it', though I dare say he may still find the primitive, if he prefers it. Nevertheless civilization has not, for once, curtailed liberty by raising walls and fences, nor infected the villages with all the trivialities of the town. People go to Arran to amuse themselves, not to be entertained. As of old, the holiday spirit is stimulated by a sense of open-air freedom not to be experienced in many holiday resorts. The island is yours.

John Joy Bell (1871-1934) *Scotland's Rainbow West* (London: Harrap, 1933)

from The Alban Goes Out
Naomi Mitchison, 1939

We set out a little before sunset,
Leaving Carradale, leaving the summer visitors,
The girls with varnished nails and beach shorts, not likely for us,
Only to be eyed and laughed with if we don't go too far:
The fishermen must be kept in their places.
We go to our place now.

Over at Arran the herring were good last night;
We cross Kilbrennan Sound in the tail of the day light,
The diesel going steady, the nets lying ready,
The Alban redded for working: that is our right.
And our neighbour boat, yon, within hail and sight.

You stand beside me, rocking as the boat rocks,
From the accustomed ankles, the knees in the grey rubber thigh-boots,
The swaying hips, dancer, oh dancer to the sea's moving, not mine now.
You hold the end of thirty fathom of wire
Dithering continuously to the water's tugging, and jerking
At the hand that waits to feel the definite patter,
Not the hard tap of mackerel, not a single fish nor a scatter,
But the feel of the whole herring shoal, oh a different matter.
The shoal you see flash on dark nights as you lie, intent, in the bows,

You can hear jump in a calm, or even smell,
Using all senses to fish the herring well.
What are you thinking of, dancer, swaying with the taut wire?
What troubles your eyes and mouth? Do you think of herring?
But he answers No, I am thinking about revolution,
And all the difficulties we will need to go through.

The wind freshens, blowing off Arran, to a jabble of sea,
Away over Cour the sunset flames out into lovely ashes,
Embers of cloud floating on a clear farness.
A whale breaks and blows, three times, across our bows,
Smoothly like the rim of a black enormous wheel, emerging and turning.
Lights in Pirnmill, lights far astern in Carradale:
Supper in the boarding-houses, fried eggs, new cake.
They have cards and whisky and wireless, papers that came with the mail,
But we are out all night with our living to make.

For all that, Colin has the tea on.

It is cozy down here, with the wee stove and the strong smell of tea,
The cut bread and the jam, the talk and jokes on the fishing,
Or some nights on the women, and all a man could be wishing;
We will get in awhile from the sound and sight of the sea.

The moon rises over Arran, creating immediately
The diamond path, older than all ancient roads.
Small lights come out, so many in one darkness:
The orderly light-houses blink, up and down the coast,
And the Carradale fleet lights up.
Has Willie had a shot yet, or Robbie?
Not yet, not yet.

We lie about easy, after the tea, in our oil-skins,
Watching the moon break through,
Gossiping quietly, speaking of market prices,
Only the wire, keeping us close to the herring,
Only the cruising engine and Sandy at the wheel,
Aware of what to do.

Naomi Mitchison (b.1897) *The Alban Goes Out* (The Raven Press, 1939)

Lochranza Brambles, etc.

Alasdair Alpin MacGregor, 1948

One of the real attractions of a sojourn at St Bride's lay in the fact that its inmates scorned the idea that one on holiday should conform with conventions as to dress and hours. There were neither door-bells nor telephone-bells to answer; and the postman came but once a day, and sometimes not even once. Frequently I wandered straight from bed to the front door in my pyjamas to accept the invitation of the warm, morning sun to loiter down to the Hollow of the Dead in my night-attire, so as to gather a pailful of brambles, or to collect sticks for firewood from among the packed debris brought down by the burn in spate, and held up in places by boulders or the low-hanging boughs of trees. Sometimes I put in half an hour's strenuous work at the pump below the house, by which water is raised to a commodious tank above it. Hard work that pump, with the sun beating on you! It made us economical with water—not that there was any shortage in the neighbourhood of St Bride's, but that all water on tap had to be pumped up laboriously from a deep well some distance below the house.

The systematic excursions from Lochranza of bramble-pickers, often ere cock-crow at Ballarie, became such a nuisance to us at St Bride's that, finally, we felt justified in pinning the following notice to the trunk of a tree at the farther end of the footbridge: 'It is earnestly requested that visitors will NOT cross this footbridge to pick brambles, as the inmates of St Bride's are vegetarians, and meanwhile are subsisting largely on the brambles growing on their own property. (signed) MacLean, Bogle, & MacGregor.'

Despite this notice, it was not until the dawn of September, when most of the holiday-makers at Lochranza had been obliged by circumstances to return to their homes on the mainland of Scotland, that again the brambles growing in the Hollow of the Dead and in the fields that once formed part of the monastery garden fell freely to our fingers, and black and luscious to our lips. At this time my staple diet consisted of brambles, and of such wholesome products as large slices of dark-stained beetroot, with a sprinkling of salt, and eaten with the fingers. How beautiful to the sight, as well as to the palate, are the natural fruits of mother earth, untainted with blood!

One sunny afternoon, as my hostess and I were on our way to the village for provisions, she saw two bulky figures moving furtively among the bramble-bushes in the Hollow of the Dead.

'Hi! What are you doing there?' she shouted at them. They did not answer; but they looked a little self-conscious, and went on with their picking. From their gait and characteristic blue jerseys, we soon realized that they were fishermen, members of the crew of a trawler or of a herring-drifter.

'Didn't you see the notice at the footbridge about the brambles?' asked my hostess, determined to go into matters thoroughly.

'No! We never seen a footbridge even,' replied one of them.

'How did you get into this field, then?' she continued.

'We just crossed the stream down there,' replied one of them, pointing in a vague sort of way to a thicket some distance off. 'We wouldn't have went into the stream, if we had kent there was a bridge.'

At this juncture it looked as though a dialogue on the existence and site of our footbridge were going to undermine our prestige, and disarm our purpose in such a way as to prevent our joining issue on the one important matter in hand—namely, that two dexterous fishermen had already stripped our bramble-bushes fairly clean, and that, while the dialogue concerning the footbridge continued, the other fisherman, with an air of complete detachment, proceeded to improve the shining hour by picking at an increasing speed. Having solved the problem as to how they had found their way into this enclosure, we discovered upon interrogation that they belonged to Campbeltown, that bad fishing conditions had resulted in their having anchored off Lochranza, that they had come off on a brambling expedition 'for something to do', that they had been told where brambles grew in plenty, and that they intended making bramble jam on their vessel whenever they returned to it.

When my hostess learned from them that they had already purchased the sugar for the jam-making, her heart melted within her. She now felt she could hardly ask them to quit. By way of compromise, therefore, she enjoined them to confine their picking to the bushes between the hedge and the side of the pathway on which they already had been operating with considerable reward. This they agreed to do.

'Have you got many?' she asked them, casting her eyes about the ground for the receptacle in which the brambles were being collected.

'Och, not many,' responded the spokesman. 'We've been working systematically along this patch for a couple of hours, and that's all we got,' and he meantime holding up to our gaze a large basket hitherto concealed from view by bracken, and containing a quantity of brambles that, from his tone, would have had us believe that he and his mate had simply been wasting their time on a profitless task. The approximate dimensions of the basket were 20 inches by 10 by 10. And it was filled to overflowing by this time.

'Working *systematically*!' shrieked my hostess, only now suddenly brought to the consciousness of how efficiently the bushes had been stripped. 'It takes four of us, picking systematically all day long, to gather as many brambles as that! What system do *you* employ? Show us your system!'

Other than that in process, no further demonstration was necessary. A few yards away, the mate with the partiality for improving the shining hour went ahead with his picking at an accelerated speed, unheeding, filling with rhythmic determination his greasy and sooty cap with his equally greasy and sooty hands, and leaving his accomplice to do the theorizing. In watching him tear the thorny runners asunder to get the more readily at the bunches of fruit, we discovered *his* system anyway. Judging by the basket-ful of berries, it was patent that to neither of these hardened seamen could bramble thorns have meant anything.

'I think we've got enough now, Sandy,' said the spokesman, who soon displayed a little embarassment on discovering that by using the word, *systematically*, he had prejudiced what otherwise might have been regarded as a casual and innocent collection of a few brambles that chanced to lie in their path. But Sandy just went on with his picking.

'I think we've got enough now, Sandy,' he repeated a moment or two later. 'We won't have enough sugar for any more.'

The additional observation about the sugar worked on the dour Sandy. Against a hint from his companion as broad as this, how could he possibly continue to pick more? Like an overgrown child suddenly prevented from enjoying himself any longer, Sandy came to heel with a surly countenance, uttering not a syllable, and casting pathetic glances towards the few bushes that still remained untouched by him. So full was his cap that he made no attempt to empty its contents into the large basket that already was sending occasional overflows down the runnels terminating where the wicker-work began, just at the base of the black, luscious mountain of berries visible to the eye.

We parted good friends with the Campbeltown fishermen. Basket and cap were filled to their utmost capacity. They could not have carried away many more brambles in any case, unless they had stowed them away internally, or in the other fellow's cap. They beamed on us with satisfaction; and we beamed on them, as they sought the high-road to Lochranza by our footbridge among the trees in the Hollow of the Dead. We wished them every success with the jam as they were on the point of disappearing from view. How could we have done otherwise in the circumstances, being cognizant of the hazard of their calling, of its uncertainties, of the prolonged discomfort it entails, of the meagre recompense the fishermen usually obtain for their labours and risks?

Despite my boast of being almost entirely devoid of a sense of acquisitiveness, I must confess that various forms of collecting gave me great satisfaction while staying at St Bride's, whether the collecting took the form of picking brambles or nuts, or of gathering mushrooms or firewood. Mushrooms of recent years have not been as plentiful hereabouts for some reason known only to the spore. But nuts abound in the woody parts of the Hollow of the Dead, and they may be gathered in fair quantities each season. Yet, they are scarcely so abundant there as in the woodlands where North Glen Sannox and the stream running through it border upon the sea. One day in mid-September a friend and I passed through North Glen Sannox to find that, merely in shaking the branches of the nut-trees, the nuts fell thick and fast to the ground. This method of dislodging ripe nuts we soon found to be wasteful, however, for the brownness of the nuts was so similar to that of the ground underneath the bushes that almost every nut thus shaken off was lost. A properly organized nut-gathering expedition into thickets such as these would have required the spreading of a couple of white sheets around the base of each bush, preparatory to shaking. Notwithstanding, with the help of a walking-stick, the handle of which I employed to pull down toward me branches otherwise out of reach, I soon filled a rucksack with brown nuts that were just on the point of being eased out of their green sockets by the ripening autumn.

*

Almost every account of Arran written in recent years, and emphasizing its attractions and amenities as a holiday resort, will persist in assuring prospective holiday-makers of the existence of such services and institutions as people really on holiday want to eschew like the very plague. I have never perused an Arran guide-book that did not extol the installation throughout the Island of an automatic telephone service, and of telephone kiosks placed at frequent intervals along its shores and among its popular holiday centres. But the crowning amenity of Arran, judging by the latest publications boosting its advantages, seems to be the promptitude with which, morning and evening, the national newspapers are obtainable throughout the Island. But who in his senses would regard the sale, in his midst, of the national newspapers as something to be desired when on holiday?

*

For me, at any rate, Arran is completely wanting in charm, although I admit it is a very beautiful Island, and one in which *most* people could spend a long and delightful holiday, and never be disillusioned, nor pine for something stranger. Never did this lack of charm impress itself upon me more than when one day I stood high above the Cock of Arran and, gazing out

North Sannox Shore by W. Noel Johnson, 1894

121

into the far north and north-west, felt the elusiveness of the hills and sea-creeks of Argyll!

The only lasting attraction Arran has for me arises from its being an island, and consequently visited by boats, since I dearly love the sea and anything that floats upon the tide. I could loiter long about a pier, if there were any likelihood of activity. One sunny afternoon, as I leaned over the balustrade of the pier at Lochranza, the puffer *Roman*, which plies between Arran and the Ayrshire ports, was unloading barrels of paraffin oil by her derrick, making hurry against a falling tide, since already her flat bottom had begun to grate. It fascinated me to watch the members of her crew working with keenness and precision at their respective tasks, remarkably skilful with their hands, sharp of eye, nimble of foot, and with all the art of ropes literally at their finger-tips. In an instant the vessel was swinging out astern with a great pother of water about her rudder, and sailing away toward the Cowal coast, a host of seamews wheeling after her.

Alasdair Alpin MacGregor *Somewhere in Scotland* (London: Robert Hale, 1948)

Servant of the Lord
Margaret Hamilton, 1950

The fair was birling, tinks, pipers, the red roof of a stall, folk and kye, chasing each other round.

Like a stone through a water-whirl, something came into their midst. A hand plucked me from the dance.

'Geordie MacCallum, think shame!'

It was Shennadale Fair Day, with the sun as canty as a tink that had sold every brush and besom he had. Island folk had good niffer for silver they'd gathered for fair day. And if the tinks took it straight to the gambling booths, the hobby-horses and the field of penny reels—well, that wasn't your blame but theirs.

My father had been saving the soul of a man by a clothing stall. Davie and I had slipped away our lone to see the world that we had been imagining since Mrs Craig first whispered to us that our father was taking us with him to the fair—only he wasn't for telling us for fear the thought would upset our daily lives and set all holiness camsteerie.

The fair was more than our imagining. We couldn't have thought of a bull breaking out and charging through the stalls till he was caught and tied by the ring on his nose. The tent-cloth of booths was ribboned, wood splintered, money sent up in the air.

We saw Effie Murdoch of Borra Free Kirk come stirring among the ruins of the Find-the-Lady stall and the Come-One-Come-All-You-Win-I-Fall. She walked like a daft bit hen that thinks her head'll get left behind if it doesn't get a poke-poke forrit with every step.

'Davie, Geordie, is it no' a judgement on them for their trade in wickedness?' says she, lifting with her stick at a bit of canvas to see was there not a penny or a maik that nobody had found yet. But I'd got the last penny from below it myself a minute before her.

We went to the dancing field and a tink wife catched me up to join the fun. Davie went running to where my father was....

Jig, jig, the reel went on without me. My father stood watching, a grey alpaca coat hanging big and loose on him. The man it belonged to came peching through the crowd, a poor bit Jew that my father had thought he was saving the soul of. But the man only wanted a sale, for he wasn't to know we'd a tailor at home that made every stitch we wore.

'A nithe fit, thir, there you are,' says he, clutching a handful of cloth at the back to make the front look right. So it was skintight at the very moment that my father was filling his lungs. A button leaped from him like a flea that smells better game.

'O ye worshippers of the golden calf,' he roared, stretching his arms to the tinks at their dancing. 'Hear me, hear me....'

But the pipers in the field had been changing their stance and they came of a sudden to where we were. Tossing their draggled ribbons, they wrung the bags to a wilder tune. A tune that strangled my father's voice, so the tinks had to laugh with what breath they had from the merciless reel.

He did not move but stood, a tall thin creature with eyes and beard glittering, while a wee man tethered him from behind, and on either side a bairn of his own watched him mouthing at folk that could not hear.

The unfair chill of a June early morning saw us going home along the shore road from my Grandma Stewart's at Shennadale where we had spent the night. Paddy, our old horse, thudded cloudily along the middle of the road, and before our eyes they were tearing the fair to bits. The merry-go-round was a scuddy skeleton, its horses lying fire-breathing to the cold empty grass. Men scratched heads over the place where the bull had done their work for them, and once the red and white cloth of a stall stood windily erect for a second before it fell wanting its wooden bones.

Our first fair was behind us and we might never live to see another. At five and six years old Davie and I were for ever expecting death, for to our smallest plans for the future our father would nail the black flag, *Gin-it-please-the-Lord-to-spare-us.*

At the turn, where the old Cross Road began, we waited for another cart to pass us. It was bigger than ours and drawn by two great Clydesdales

Lamlash Agricultural Show, August 1954 (photograph by Robert Walker)

with twin white stars on their foreheads and their tails still plaited with white and blue ribbons. It was Jamieson of the Knowe in Borra, and his five buirdly daughters were with him, as well as two calves resigned in sacks, and a kist to hold the fairings that six of them had bought.

Lizzie, the second and boldest daughter, jumped from the cart as it passed us. Her petticoats, every one of them, took longer to come down than she did, but she only laughed and came over to us. 'Weel, Geordie...weel, Davie...' says she in her voice that matched her bigness.

The two of us, sitting on the edge of the cart, would have answered, but as we opened our mouths she reached up and shoved into them two such dawds of tough jean from the fair that I for one couldn't have said 'I'm fin' if it was the queen and all her ladies that had Weel Geordie'd me.

But maybe they were better than that, the Jamieson lassies in their Sunday braws. Douce brown and blue frocks they had, but half a hundred petticoats among them, and bonnets and ribbons all waving to match their laughing and their shouts that came back to us, 'Weel, Geordie...weel, Davie...' till their cart was away on the hill.

My father was not ill-pleased. He even drove the cart half-way up the hill before he remembered that we should get down to save Paddy from pulling our weight. The toffee, still big in our mouths, was rounded and warm by then and we could shift it to give room to our tongues.

But we weren't for saying much there in the glen with the sun not right at its work, and far below us the dark-tree smothered burn where kelpies and bocans had their ploys.

If you can see the map of Scotland as a daft angry sheep, you will find Ramma to the west, at the bottom of the half-circle made by the churning forelegs. An island twenty miles long by ten-about wide, except where she is bunched together by the glen with the old Cross Road going through it. To the south of that, below the waist you'd think, there is a line of bens that they call the Sleeping Warrior for the look it has of a giant stretched out with a helmet on. On that part of the island the laird has his castle; Sir William Crawford it was in my day.

The folk that scratch the land for a living do it mostly along the shore. There was never more than a handful of crofts eating inland at either end of the Cross Road: Shennadale to the east and Borra to the west. Farther in you would find whiles a broken-down cottage where folk had lived once, but the earth gave no signs of their striving for it against the peaty muir....

Climbing the Cross Road when you were the size of Davie and me was like swallowing a long dose of oil, not knowing whether the spoonful of sugar that had always been waiting for you before would be there this time as well. The sugar was the peak of the road.

Hands clamped together and sweat breaking out on us, we ran, watching my father and Paddy go from us round a bend and thinking we never might see them again.

We reached the top. The sun, squandering itself when it wasn't needed, lit the glen. Bracken reached up with sweet young arms and trees took their bright separate greens as the water jinked among them.

But we were hurtling ourselves into the cart again, as the down-going road rushed to meet Paddy's up-trained feet. And far away, before the islets set their hallmark on the distant silver sea, lay Cailleach, our home.

Margaret Hamilton (1915-1972) *Bull's Penny* (MacGibbon & Kee, 1950)

Arran Villages
George Blake, 1952

Brodick is obviously a West Highland hamlet that has grown up under the patronage of townsfolk, mainly of the middle-classes, but on a bright day, when the young people are milling along the shore road in their coloured garments and colour is blazing on the hillsides round about, one gets the feeling of an element almost Mediterranean in the scene. Here there are golf and tennis to be played; here you may swim and go boating or sea-fishing; here may be your angling or mountaineering base. But there are no fun fairs, no helter-skelters. At the height of the season a mobile cinema may operate twice a week, alternating with free-for-all dances in the public hall. The rest is as natural, even primitive, as it may be in the 20th Century. The compromise is singularly happy.

Every visitor to Arran automatically goes round the island at least once. The bus and taxi services are ample. Assuming the vehicle to be heading south-about the next port of call is Lamlash, a village rather larger than Brodick but hardly its match in situation, style and tone. Before this point is reached, however, a traverse of one of Arran's exciting passes must be made. No road on this island can be anything but narrow and tortuous; no native driver is anything but pragmatical in his approach to the use of clutch and gears. Thus even this brief journey of four miles or so can be an exciting affair as the road winds under trees, over mosses flecked with lint, and the vehicle must slow down continually to let another pass or allow a Blackface ewe and her lamb or even a Highland cow to rise at leisure from their resting places on the warm tarmac.

The descent into Lamlash is spectacular not for any special dizziness of the descent, steep though that may be, but because one suddenly sees how splendidly the high hump of the Holy Isle at once encloses and embellishes the very fine natural harbour of Lamlash Bay.

Some people feel that Lamlash is too warmly enclosed by the tall island on the seaward side and the high hills inland. These hills crowd closely on the village, but again there are twin glens, Benlister and Monamore, to lighten the little patch of flat green land by the sea. The bay has the largest sweep of any on Arran, and it is completely protected from all winds save those from two fine points of the compass. Especially before the First War it was much used by the Royal Navy, and at one period of post-war shortage the longshoremen of the district turned an honest penny by trawling for the tons of coal that had been lost overside in the process of bunkering.

Lamlash village is much less compact than Brodick, less distinguished in its architecture and lay-out. It seems to straggle, and for some not easily discernible reason it has always tended to attract holidaymakers on subtly lower income levels than that of those faithful to its more fashionable neighbours. It may be surmised that it is a much older establishment than either Brodick or Whiting Bay—a surmise well-rooted in its distinction as a harbour of refuge—and that it was, as it were, slightly industrialised before its neighbours waxed on the tourist trade. It remains a very pleasant place on a bay of singular beauty and nobility. The enclosure of salt water between the green foothills of the Arran mainland and the grey screes of the Holy Isle has at once the boldness of the sea proper and the charm of a fjord.

*

The character of Whiting Bay differs distinctly from that of its neighbours. It is less cosy, so to speak, than Brodick and Lamlash, much less a natural harbour. The curve of the bay is rather flat; the exposure is to the

126

Whiting Bay, the Pier and Holy Isle

east. In a sense it consists of two bays separated by the mild promontory from which the pier extends. Both have patches of fine yellow sand, and as the name suggests there is good fishing in the offshore waters, and there are flounders to be speared over the sand inshore.

This wide bay is partly overlapped by the southern tip of the Holy Isle, the white lighthouse buildings always startling against the greys and greens of scree and bracken, but the general aspect is open to the wide, occasionally wild stretches of the outer Firth, and all the considerable sea traffic of a great harbour is to be seen passing up and down the fairway for ocean-going vessels. In a word: as distinct from those of Brodick and Lamlash, the atmosphere of Whiting Bay has an oceanic quality.

The human settlements along these pleasant shores are extensive in terms of mere length and considerably varied as to architecture. Here is clearly another case of a tiny hamlet having been developed by forces from outside itself; for Whiting Bay was never a small capital like Brodick nor a harbour like Lamlash. The dynamics were provided by the industrial folk of the mainland, always seeking their ways of escape, and it is of mild interest that in the closely-marked scale of social values rigidly applied on an island mainly patronised by the middle-middle and lower-middle classes—and very little by the working folk, for fairly obvious reasons—Whiting Bay was for a long time, but a time now passing, regarded as having more 'tone' than its neighbours.

Blackwaterfoot is a simple enough little place, stone built and clean. For its own sake the traveller would hardly linger here. But there is a view, and there is a beach; and, above all, the most skilful use has been made of the natural features of the riparian lands running northwards. These are links of fine, hard turf and make an excellent golf course. Against a range of low cliffs hard by the clubhouse runs a series of tennis courts. On a fine summer's day this aggregation of elements has the air of a planned Lido or country club, and that for the most interesting reason of all.

Blackwaterfoot is, as a holiday resort, virtually governed by the regular summer visitors from Glasgow, Paisley, Greenock and parts adjoining, who form what is in fact a local improvement association. Here, in this remote corner of the remarkable Isle of Arran, there has been established a convention rather more powerful than those of the natives. Here is a club in effect; and as we shall see later on, the social structure of Arran is based to a remarkable extent upon the needs and demands of its summer patrons, mostly of the industrial professional middle classes.

Lochranza at the north-eastern corner of the island has none of the glitter of Blackwaterfoot. It is a more real sort of place, so to speak. The loch itself is barely a mile in length and just about half as much in breadth, and it is steeply enclosed by high hills: a cosy little harbour. A feature of this harbour is a gravelly spit which nearly cuts off the head of the bay. This is a pleasant feature when the tide is in: hardly so pleasant at the ebb when it dries out in mud, in spite of the interesting ruins of an old castle upon it. When the herring fleets of the outer Firth were much larger than they are now, Lochranza was a fishing port of some little consequence, and the graceful, brown-sailed smacks would be moored by the dozen behind the castle in the off-hours. But the herring fishing has gone from Arran, concentrated in just a few mainland ports, and Lochranza in consequence wears something of the air of a small seaport turned part holiday resort and part a place of refuge for retired sea captains and chief engineers.

As a holiday resort it cannot compete in popularity with Brodick or Whiting Bay, for so its position, its difficult communications and its relatively austere character dictate. Lochranza has, of course, its devotees, as what humblest hamlet of Arran has not? What was once its inn or hotel became a Scottish Youth Hostel, and hikers and mountaineers are much in evidence in the season. The detached traveller may probably be most interested to see the place as a sort of sport from the general pattern of the island: as it were, something Scandinavian and antique, slightly rough and cold within an agglomeration that has so many gentle and even elegant passages.

*

This island had once upon a time its considerable fishing industry. It still has a useful farming industry. Its chief industry, however, has become that of catering for the holidaymaker.

Once the small wars had died down with the Jacobite failure in 1745,

Arran must have been a poor sort of place in the economic sense. Below the ennobled gentry there can have been but one or two bonnet lairds, or considerable farmers, and below these again nothing but crofters and fishermen on the barest level of subsistence. We may imagine that the native economy might have improved with general progress in the early 19th Century, but there can be no doubt at all that it got its chief stimulus from the development of the steamboat on the shores of the inner Firth and on the banks of the Clyde Ship-Channel up to Glasgow.

This stimulus was, as it were, naturally selective. The smallest and earliest steamboats could not safely compass the voyage into nearly open waters; few industrial wage-earners of the early 19th Century could afford the fares. Arran was thus fated to be a paradise of the more prosperous industrial classes. The well-to-do merchants came first and built their 'marine villas'. The slightly less affluent followed to build or buy their seaside cottages. Conditions subtly changing, decent middle-class folk from Clydeside took to the regular renting of furnished houses for a month 'at the Coast'.

A local industry was born thus. All over Arran there were to be seen, even five years after the end of the Second World War, villas, farmhouses and cottages with tarred shacks behind or beside them, into which their owners retired for the season while the visitors from Glasgow or parts adjacent occupied the main premises, paid their substantial furnished rents and provided a considerable proportion of the island's internal revenue.

Even if there was an inevitable levelling-out of economic and social forces under Britain's first effective Labour Government, Arran strangely remained the shrine of a cult, largely middle-class in structure. Year after year the same families went to the same hotel or boarding house or rented the same villa. You were faithful to Brodick and despised Lamlash, or you were one of the Blackwaterfoot crowd, looking down your nose on any patron of the eastern bays. Cliques and snobberies abounded; within the Arran cult there was among the young people, so happily circumstanced, much lovemaking and engaging in the serious business of marriage. One has known of three generations of a Glasgow family finding its mates on its own social levels in the long and lovely evenings of the North on an island singularly blessed.

A novelist with the right sardonic touch could have a lot of fun with the doings of a suburban Glasgow family on its annual holiday on Arran. He or she would still have to account for the superb quality of the scene, the setting and the circumstances; also, a much more difficult matter, the loving fidelity of a great number of sensible people to an island in the fairway of the outer Firth of Clyde.

George Blake (1893-1961) *The Firth of Clyde* (London: Collins, 1952)

Arran Burn
A Poem for Television
Robert McLellan, 1965

Look whaur the mist reiks aff the split craigs
In the hairt o the desolation o creation,
Whaur the primal convulsions o fire and ice
And doun the years the weir and teir o the wather,
Wind, rain, frost, thaw and drouth,
Hae wrocht in the end this unremarkable miracle,
That beauty is born whaur the corbies craik daith.

See alchemy o warm air on the chill stane
And the draps seep through the screes to the corrie heid
And runnels gurgle whaur the gresses growe green.

Sune nou the stags that graze quaitly thegither,
Whan the first rowan spills its reid seed,
Will ken in the nostril the hinds lang forgotten
And the stir o the rut in the unbiddable bluid,
But the sturt and the struggle bide on the drap o the berry,
And for a while yet their tines haud nae threat.

Gress will gie them flesh till the first o the frosts,
Syne dearth will drive them to the corrie lip
And the burn's white streak draw them doun
Straucht as a gled's dive into the glen heid
Whaur the cowed hinds will gather to thole the inevitable
Jealous discipline o the antlered maister.

But first the leaf maun faa, and till the turn
Nae male unease will echo frae the hills,
But the gill cry peace abune the wide muir
And the linns utter benedictions by ancient memorials.
For here were laid the banes o the isle's Adam.
Here the god and faither o his kindred
Lay his days o daith by his crock o meal,
And in the mysterious nicht drank his druid milk.
Nou the broun breckans crown the stanes
Lang herried by the viking and the scholar,
And the banes that moulder in the rufeless chaulmer
Were pykit by a black-back in the spring.

Here the yowe that cried her desolation
Grazes again wi her lost lamb forgotten,
And like the hinds about the brae abune her
Draws to the rut and the lang winter cairry,
For in a field by the fanks the tups are fed wheat.

But the leaf maun faa first, and the cauld blast
Scatter its gowden shouer on the linn pules
Abune the troots that gether for the floods,
Plump wi their raun, and restless for the run,
And the lowp, and the splash, and the bore through the spate
To the slack o some runnel lost in the lang ling.
There in the graivel the hen will rowe her redd,
And spill her raun, and the cock shed his milt.

But first the leaf maun faa, and till the rains
The linns will roar nae thunder ower the muirs
Nor the last stanes o the lost magic circle
Trummle on the bog abune their tummelt maiks.
Here played the bairns o the isle's Adam,
The sun their guidsir and the yird their grannie,
At ring-a-rosie in the wame o time,
And day followed the nicht, and spring the winter,
And whan the seed was sawn the hairst was gethert,
And the miracle o birth defeated daith.
Nou the ring is broken and the rite forgotten,
And the sun and the yird are nae mair sacred,
And the nicht and the winter are still to come.

But the god that followed made aa things guid.
The sun and the yird are still in wadlock
And the leaf maun faa still and the berries scatter
On the pules aneth the linns whaur the troots are plump.
For look abune the burn in this lown hallie.
See this sunken waa smoored in breckans.
Here a bald abbat brocht a martyr's bane
And spak in Gaelic o the risen Christ,
And wrote His passion in a book o skins,
And lit His haly rude, and rang His bell;
And whan the bell was rung the douce disciples
Pat heuk and flail aside, and stane and divot,
To bend their knees in their first kirk o sticks,
And chaunt in Latin for the sauls o sinners.
Nou this bit rickle is aa their memorial

And the yowes graze wi nae man in sicht,
Though Christ's bell rings yet, in the glen fute.

Come nou to the muir's lost clachans.
See whaur the ash leans ower the lang shallas
And the gress is green by the forgotten ford.
Yonder dwalt folk that were sib to the fairies.
Adam their forebeir, watchin by nicht
Frae his wee stane hoose aneth his hillock,
Saw them won frae the stane ring by the men o the rude
And pey their siller penny to the viking
And their merk to the Norman, their sheepskin chief.

By their darg on this muir in their run rigs
They peyed their rent and held their banes thegither,
And nae disaster o wat, frost or drouth,
Nae blight or sickness in corn or beast,
Nae human epidemic or injustice,
Nor ony hazard o their baron's wars,
Sword or fire, or famine efter pillage,
Broke the lang line o their succession.

Yet they gaed in the end to make wey for sheep.

See the yowes graze nou wi nae man in sicht
And the breckans creep doun to the auld gortchens.
Seeds o thistles drift ower tummelt lintels
To sills and hearth-stanes on flairs o ling
In the grey ghaists o Gaelic byres and kitchens.
Through the tuim winnock hear the hish o the shallas
And the souch o the ash in the wind frae the balloch.
Wi the lambs and the whaups gane this is aa their elegy,
Though gulls may wail whiles ower some broken banes.

But the burn draps nou at the muir's edge,
And here in this deep den it slides and tummles
Ower jummelt rocks aneth heich hingin shaws
To holes and neuks in countless pules and runnels.
Doun and doun it rummles and chaunts and chinners
Aneth the nuits that ripen on the hazels
And the berries o haw and slae and the hips o the rose.
Spume rains aff the fulyery o birks
On yella taid-stules amang rotten sticks
Aside the pule aneth the fernie faa

Whaur the first o the saumon frae the firth lie baffled.
Cock and hen they ken they will fling in vain
Against this waa till the gales roar again
And the rains swall the torrent and gie them grip.
Here till the floods come is the end o their epic.
Atween here and the burn mooth they will dree their weird
In a back-end o hide and seek wi the otters,
For they tae, dug and bitch, are up frae the firth,
And wi the drap o the berry will hae their holt howkit,
And their spring whalps safe in the wame for the winter.

Whaur they play nae saumon is safe,
But they lie low nou till the daurk faas,
For oot on the brae they hear the shepherd whistle
As he tents his tups in the field abune the ferm,
And they ken his collie is back aff the hill.

Nou look whaur the burn rins oot to the heid o the holms.

Here was a kirk was first a simple clauchan,
And syne the chapel o a Romish saunt,
And syne the hoose o the grim god o Knox.
Here the folk o the lost run-rig clachans
Forgied their neibors' debts for generations
And heard their banns cried and their sins admonished
And cam for consolation in seikness and daith.
Nou their bairns bide, and their names, cut in stane,
Though wind and wather play havoc ilk winter
And the face o the auld saunt is weirin awa.

But the burn winds nou in the braid holms,
Slawly and saftly by fields in hedges
And bien ferms white in the beild o their trees.
Here fat kye suckle ither mithers' cauves
And milkers staun heavy wi hingin udders.
Coles o hey and stooks o corn wait the liftin
And neeps and kail swall for the days aheid.
Aa thocht nou is for the lang winter dearth.
The folk o the ferms hoard like squirrels.
Hey is piled heich to the barn rufe
And ricks are thackit against the rain wi rashes.
In the wat and cauld to come fodder maun be handie
To the byre and the cauf shed and the bull's box.

And aye the burn rins nearer to the firth,
Windin by wuids nou and cottage gairdens,
Whaur guidsirs lift tatties or gether aipples,
And roun by the sawmill, whaur wuidmen cut posts,
And strainers and streitchers and stobs for fences,
And rafters and runners, and framin and sarkin,
And props for coal-pits, and logs for fires.

Syne doun by the backs o the villas and bungalows
And the pub and the private hotels and the tearoom,
By nettles and dockens and tangles o brambles
And cowps o auld cans and aa sorts o bottles,
Sauce bottles, wine bottles, whisky and gin bottles,
Chemists' and druggists' and doctors' bottles,
And torn and dune hot watter bottles,
And auld airn bed-ends, and sewers, and drains.

And syne, in the end, ablow the shore road brig
And oot across the links by green and bunker
To the braid bay o boats and bathin boxes.
Here, efter the steer and bustle o the simmer,
Aa is idle. Alang the strand,
Laved by the lazy waves o the flood tide,
The sated whaup and pyet bide the turn,
Dozin in dizzens on their lang thin shanks
Aside the serried gulls, aa silent nou,
Wi feathers fluffed and beaks sunk in their breists.
Efter the scrabble is their hour o rest,
And where is peace was ance a simmer's bedlam.
For here at the sun's turn were folk in boat-loads:
Faithers o faimlies wi rugs and deck-chairs,
And mithers wi picnic and baby baskets;
And lassies wi records and baby transistors
And towels and sun-tan and bits o bikinis;
And laddies wi harpoons and fins and goggles;
And toddlers wi reels and lines and sinkers
And hooks and nets and spades and buckets;
And crawlers in harness and plastic panties;
Girners and greiters and yellers and skrechers
And tooters and whistlers and roarers and lauchers
And lollipop lickers and sweetie sookers
And waders and splashers and dookers and divers
And haddie and fluke and poddlie fishers
And snoozers and snorers, and litter leavers.

134

Nou the clean bay lies white aneth the hills,
And aa is silent, till the lane boatman,
Draggin his dinghies abune the line o the wrack,
Opens his tractor throttle. The seabirds rise,
And wheel across the bay in sudden fricht,
And the whaup's twa winter notes stir memories
O days by cairn and clachan on the muir
Whan its spring sang was uttered haill and clear;
The perfect elegy for the lost folk o the glen.

Robert McLellan *Sweet Largie Bay and Arran Burn: Two Poems in Scots* (Preston: Akros Publications, 1977)

Victim Running

Archie Roy, 1968

As I neared the pillar post-box at the junction of the Shiskine and Machrie Roads, a grey Minivan catapulted up the Machrie Road from the Glaistir Bridge. Even as I rammed down the accelerator I remembered a similar van in the yard at Carradale House and the computer in my mind gave its comments: distance from Carradale House along the Machrie Road to post-box is three miles—distance from the Doon along the Shiskine Road is six miles—they must have belted along—Leighton must have phoned within three minutes.

The needle climbed to sixty-five as I dived down the last slope and ripped past the stone pillar box on to the String. My lead increased as the Mini slowed to make the left hand turn. But I couldn't hold it on the twisting narrow road for the Mini was not only more manoeuvrable than the ton and a half of Armstrong-Siddeley but also had a better driver. In the next thirty seconds the lead dwindled noticeably even before we began the climb up the String with its sharp corners that would certainly let them get right behind me. They couldn't pass if I kept to the road centre and they couldn't tumble the heavy Siddeley off the road to go crashing down the sloping sides of the Glen into the river but I'd no doubt they could put a bullet in me or a tyre before we reached the top.

My logic overcame the seductive illusion of security the car interior gave me and at the last possible moment I jammed both feet on clutch and brake. The speed fell from seventy to well under thirty in a scream of fusing rubber and in the rear mirror I saw the Mini shorten the gap by eighty feet. I raised my feet, stopped fighting the wheel, swung it hard left to the full extent of its lock and felt the big car swing off the road on two wheels and dive down the steep, almost hidden farm road leading to Monyquil. In the mirror I saw the Mini shoot past, its driver obviously braking. Feeling sweat bands trickle down my forehead, I drove along the stony track, crossed the narrow wooden bridge over the Machrie water with a rattling of planks, then followed the track between the fields up to the farm house. The Mini appeared two hundred yards behind me. I put the Siddeley on to the second bridge over the Garbh Allt stream, ran it along to a farm gate and stopped. If they had a rifle I was done for. I jumped out, climbed the gate and sprinted for the rising grassy slopes that bordered the stream. Breasting the first rise I turned and looked backwards and downwards. The grey Mini had stopped behind the Siddeley. Two men had got out. A third stayed in the driver's seat. After a short discussion the two started off after me. Neither had rifles.

I began to move upwards again over the uneven tufted grass slope. The going was comparatively easy, the springy vegetation letting one's feet sink in until the tufts came to mid-shin. There were bog-wet patches and quite soon my shoes, socks and the legs of my trousers were as sodden as before. I found myself settling down to a fast, bouncing pace determined by the nature of the terrain and my need to keep at least three hundred yards ahead of my pursuers. They tried to run several times and I had to do likewise but the ground soon discouraged such attempts. They were now committed, as I had intended, to tiring me or sneaking up when the surface permitted.

By the time we had gone a mile towards the north, I could tell which of the two was the greater danger. The smaller and stockier man wore a neat dark blue lounge suit; he tended to lag behind and once I saw him sit on a rock outcrop, shoulders hunched, his hands on his knees, for the best part of a minute while he got his breath back. The other in striped tee-shirt and faded blue jeans, was in better condition. I continued to climb, still following the burn, moving almost due north towards the lower, rock-bestrewn slopes of Ben Nuis.

By now I felt hot and semi-exhausted, my shirt and singlet sticking to the small of my back while streams of sweat coursed down my burning face. The only sound I heard was the regular heavy in-and-out breath in my open mouth, as if some phantom doctor accompanying me kept ordering me to take deep breaths. I wondered what the third man in the Mini was doing. Probably reporting back to Leighton. With that thought I changed direction slightly, now aiming for the western shoulder of Ben Nuis. The ground began to steepen and more and more of it became composed of outcrop and broken rock with bell heather, blaeberry plants and tough knotted grass between. I had now come two and a half miles and climbed a thousand feet from the place where I'd abandoned the Armstrong-Siddeley.

Glancing back, I saw that Tee-shirt was attempting a spurt. He managed to close the gap to one hundred and fifty yards before a faint shout from Lounge Suit, now three hundred yards behind, made him slow up and sink on to a rock. I kept on, now scrambling over the lower part of the shoulder of the Ben, its huge granite bulk heaping up to my right.

To the left the ground fell away sharply down to the distant Iorsa Water in its meanders over the sea-green bottom of Glen Iorsa. Beyond the Glen, Chalmadale and Ben Bharrain soared up, blotting out the far distant Mull of Kintyre. To the south-west, the Mull was visible, down past Davaar Island to where Sanda Isle lay darkly on the grey-blue horizon.

Tee-shirt was waiting until Lounge Suit caught up. Very gratefully, I slowed up, just moving forward, for my heart was pounding and I would have given anything to lie prone for five minutes. I transferred my wallet, pen, diary and keys to my trousers pockets and threw away my tweed jacket. My tie went into my pocket. I should have done it when I left the car.

I was now climbing up into the bleak, granite heart of the island where the great ridges and peaks rise in their most impressive aspects, desolate, tumbled, old. The silence was broken only by my harried breathing or the sudden startled whirring flutter of the occasional grouse's wings or the cold splash of a spring tumbling down over wet lichened rocks on the side of Ben Nuis. For mile upon mile on all sides there was not a single human habitation. Twice I spotted herds of red-coated deer. In one case, a solitary stag, his antlers held high, lorded it amid a dozen hinds. The second group consisted of thirty or more stags.

I glanced back. Leighton's men were on the move again. I began to work my way northwards along the difficult forty-five degree slope of Ben Nuis. The whole slope consisted of a semi-scree of irregular, granite blocks from loaf-sized cubic boulders to megalithic slabs, all jumbled together as they had broken and avalanched down the slope. There were patches a few yards across where decomposed granite rubble and rotting vegetation had enabled a tough matting of thickly woven heather and grass to grow over the naked rock.

It took an hour to cover just over a mile of this treacherous ground in my exhausted state. My pursuers, I was satisfied to see, were now at least three hundred yards back and still keeping to my path. This they had to do since they had no idea whether I meant to strike up the slope of Ben Nuis or veer north-west downwards to the floor of Glen Iorsa in a desperate effort to break out to Loch Ranza. I felt grateful that I had explored these moors and mountains as a boy and was still fond of walking.

I now dropped a couple of hundred feet in the next half mile where the western slope of Ben Nuis becomes the western slope of Ben Tarsuinn. The ground was flatter in front of me but shot up more steeply to the right in great granite sheets, eroded and split by millennia of weathering, to the saddle between the Bens. I braced myself for I was nearing the point where I hoped to get rid of Tee-shirt and Lounge Suit. Roger the Dodger, I thought. I cheered myself a little by considering their quandary. If Leighton and Co. hadn't found the gun I had thrown away, they had to assume I was armed. Tee-shirt and Lounge Suit had probably been warned about this and it could be the reason they hadn't closed in yet, though I suspected and hoped it simply meant that they were even more exhausted than I was. They also faced the fact that although their Mini driver knew I had lit out for the hills, he had no idea what area I was in now. I stumbled, almost fell and recovered myself. Again I had a sudden terrifying vision of breaking a leg and lying there while they closed in to finish me off. I felt sickness well up within me and a metallic taste contaminated my mouth when I recalled coming across a dead sheep on these very same hills years ago after the carrion crows had been at it for a week. I steadied myself and looked round.

Ahead of me the giant shoulder of Ben Tarsuinn rose, encumbered with thousands of granite blocks. To the left it swept downwards more and more steeply to the Iorsa Valley. To the right it rose five hundred feet to the summit, 2,700 feet high. Beyond it I knew the ground fell sharply into a hollow at the base of A'Chir Ridge with a visible path running up the side to the top of the jagged, deeply notched ridge.

I stepped across a tiny burn, knelt down and cupped my hands in the freezing water. As I drank, the cold liquid chilling my gullet, the wet from the heather and moss soaked my knees. I glanced back over the dripping bowl of my fingers and saw that they were having another conference. Lounge Suit pointed backwards, Tee-shirt shook his head angrily. By no means an academic discussion. I sat down on a boulder and rested my back against a convenient block behind it. For a few seconds I felt much worse, my legs quivery, my lungs raw, my mouth now an inner core of melting ice in the furnace of my face. I splashed my face with water and wiped it. Sweat started out immediately after. My feet were beginning to hurt and in two places at least developing blisters were heralding their painful advent. I thought I knew the terms of the discussion. If Lounge Suit went back down to Monyquil he could tell the others where we were but (a) it would take *him*—I glanced at my watch—good heavens, at least three hours to deliver the message to Garcia unless they were on their way up and (b) it would diminish their ability to stop me breaking back if I intended to repeat my tactics at the Doon.

My breathing was back to normal. I rose and started off towards the shoulder ahead that ran across my route. I moved steadily until I was on top with the broad ridge surging away up to the peak on my right and could now see down into the gully between Tarsuinn and A'Chir Ridge. I went on, descending fifty feet or so until the shoulder hid me from sight. Immediately it did so I turned right and began to scramble as fast as I could over the green-brown tufts and white-wash hued blocks. I climbed on, rapidly getting more and more exhausted in a supreme effort to reach the top of Ben Tarsuinn before the others came over the ridge. The last two hundred feet almost beat me. I dropped every fifty feet or so on to the nearest granite block to drag oxygen into my tormented lungs before clawing my way upwards again. Still there was no sign of the others. I made a final endeavour and collapsed in the shelter of the gigantic tabular masses of granite that lie sheet upon weathered sheet in great prismatic forms on the edge of the vertical eastern face of Ben Tarsuinn.

By now, I thought, they would be arriving on top of the ridge and would really be in trouble. Apart from the hundreds of blocks I could be hiding behind, they would discover there were three or four widely different routes I could have taken, all of them possessing plenty of cover. If they were townbred, too, as I suspected, the scene before them could only engender confusion and dismay. Beyond A'Chir Ridge a maze of great precipices fell away to the depths from blue-grey towering crests of naked rock crowned with massive blocks, up to ten feet thick, forming tumbled and ruined stone walls. Their confusion would be increased by the way the jagged ridges separated valleys, any one of which could have been my goal, if they could only distinguish the routes over and through the majestic disorder before them.

I guessed they would cast about for a time, very cagily, in case I had any idea of ambushing them. This procedure being fruitless, they might finally agree to split up, one continuing the search (almost certainly Tee-shirt), the other making the irritating and exhausting trek back along the western slopes of Ben Tarsuinn and Ben Nuis before descending across the moor to meet the others coming up from Monyquil. The only possibility that disturbed me was that they might immediately climb after me to the crest of Ben Tarsuinn in an effort to spot me below. I decided it was time to withdraw. Run, do not walk, to the nearest exit.

To anyone reaching the summit of either Ben Tarsuinn or Ben Nuis for the first time, it comes as a surprise to discover that the crest is broad and grassy for most of the way with the living rock bursting through here and there in great heaped-up walls and that there is a well-defined though uneven and winding path among these walls and steps. The left hand edge is precipitous, requiring real mountaineering skill; on the right the shoulder dives smoothly over in scree slopes down past the level we had so laboriously worked our way along. I had in fact conned Tee-shirt and Lounge Suit for it is possible to *run* most of the way along the path at the eastern edge of the broad top. If I had been fresh I could by this route have reached the southern end of Ben Nuis ridge in a quarter of an hour or less. In the condition I was in it took longer. I also made full use of the available cover and although I kept looking backwards I saw no sign of pursuit. When I stopped to rest on the steep slope looking north-east over the wide hollow between Ben Nuis and Ben a'Chliabhain I felt certain that I'd left them behind, cloaked with cursing as with a garment.

Archie Roy (b.1924) *Deadlight* (London: John Long, 1968)

Coach Tour and Locals

George Bruce, 1969

'Sunset-red rhododendrons—
to your left.' You look
with one neck. 'To your right
alone on the rock in the blue bay—
a solitary heron, the emblem
of Arran.' At the top of the pass,
'over there now hidden in the mist—
the white stag of Arran.'
With one head you look at nothing.

The little waves lap their feet
on the golden shore.
They look at nothing.

Success is to look
at nothing
be neither
yesterday nor tomorrow.

Yesterday the *Girl Jean*
running for tomorrow
with a fair catch
off Holy Isle,
struck an iron sea.
It took her and her crew
to the trash of the abyss.

Death was not their due.

George Bruce (b.1909) *Lines Review* 30, October 1969. Reprinted in *Collected Poems* (Edinburgh University Press, 1971)

Isle of Arran

Alistair Reid, 1978

Where no one was was where my world was stilled
into hills that hung behind the lasting water,
a quiet quilt of heather where bees slept,
and a single slow bird in circles winding
round the axis of my head.

Any wind being only my breath, the weather
stopped, and a woollen cloud smothered the sun.
Rust and a mist hung over the clock of the day.
A mountain dreamed in the light of the dark
and marsh mallows were yellow for ever.

Still as a fish in the secret loch alone
I was held in the water where my feet found ground
and the air where my head ended,
all thought a prisoner of the still sense—
till a butterfly drunkenly began the world.

Alastair Reid (b.1926) *Weathering* (Edinburgh: Canongate, 1978)

Flying Over Arran
Robin Fulton, 1979

Fields I got lost in.
I retched on the raw smells beneath
imperfect grain, dreamt
of cornflowers filling the sky.

In dreams I've commuted there,
always on time, shaking
off travellers' jinxes,
opening doors, turning corners—
as if a sun-warmed stone
had kept warm for forty years.

Passing where I was born
four decades later and
thirty thousand feet higher,
New World sweat in my pores,
was not what I expected.
Pale micro-fields in a haze.
I take a picture down through space.
Only an outline shows.
Something light-years away,
a blow-up, cupped in my hand.

Robin Fulton (b.1937) *Poetry Review* January 1979. Reprinted in *Selected Poems* (Edinburgh: Macdonald, 1980)

Arran Haiku

Robin Fulton, c.1980

Crushed grass in the thirties. An
extinct bird, Avro Anson,
drills soft clouds over Arran.

Bharrain, Bhreac, Tarsuinn,
Nuis, Goat Fell. They made
huge clouds trickle down quiet glens.

Whiting Bay. Full cups
of rhododendron
waited to be touched and spilt.

Corrie. A name heard
like a bell from lips
of wet home-coming adults.

Blackwaterfoot. Grey
hulking warships, short-
lived cathedrals in the mist.

Shiskine. Black and white keys trained
at Mozart. Wet colours ran
down tall streaming manse windows.

Robin Fulton c.1980

Bungalow Road, Lamlash

Siva in Lamlash

Hamish Whyte, 1982

Pine cones burn
tongues of fire
charred voices in the flame:
eighty four thousand mouths
ash for one head.

Smirr drifts across the bay
like smoke.

There is a rainbow
at the foot
of Bungalow
Road.

Hamish Whyte (b.1947) *Cencrastus* 8, Spring 1982

Arran Potatoes

Edwin Morgan, 1985

Consul	is not quite the clean one.
Signet	is a hot one.
Pilot	is all eyes.
Rose	is a croquette.
Viking	is a masher.
Peak	is pure granite chips.
Comrade	is in his old jacket.
Victory	is piping skirlie.
Banner	is a patch.
Comet	is a trail of peelings.
Crest	is crisp.
Chief	is Raleigh the Reiver.

Edwin Morgan (b.1920) *The Glasgow Magazine 7*, Winter 1985/86

The Sleeping Warrior

Iain Banks, 1986

One of his earliest memories was of mountains, and an island. His mum and dad, his youngest sister and he had gone to Arran for their holidays; he had been three years old. As the steamer paddled down the glittering river towards the distant blue mass of the island, his dad had pointed out the Sleeping Warrior; the way the mountain range at the north end of the island looked like a helmed soldier, lying over the landscape, mighty and fallen. He'd never forgotten that sight, or the medley of accompanying sounds; calling gulls, the slap-slap of the steamer's paddles; an accordion band playing somewhere aboard, people laughing. It also gave him his first nightmare: his mum had to wake him up, in the bed he was sharing with his sister in the guest house; he'd been crying and whimpering. In his dream, the great stone warrior had woken up, and come slowly, terribly, crushingly, to kill his parents.

Iain Banks (b.1954) *The Bridge* (Macmillan, 1986)

Coire Fhionn Lochan

Thomas A. Clark, 1990

lapping of the little waves
breaking of the little waves
spreading of the little waves
idling of the little waves

rippling of the little waves
settling of the little waves
meeting of the little waves
swelling of the little waves

trembling of the little waves
dancing of the little waves
pausing of the little waves
slanting of the little waves

tossing of the little waves
scribbling of the little waves
lifting of the little waves
sparkling of the little waves

leaping of the little waves
drifting of the little waves
running of the little waves
splashing of the little waves

Thomas A. Clark (b.1944) (Moschatel Press, 1990)

Holy Isle

Alison Prince, 1991

A few weeks ago a fair-haired girl called Fiona came to lunch. She was doing a research project as part of her course at Glasgow University, trying to find out how Arran people would feel about Buddhists buying Holy Isle.

When a very polite voice on the telephone asked a few weeks later if some Buddhists could come and stay, I'd almost forgotten my absent-minded offer of accommodation. I tend to ask anyone who seems pleasant and agreeable.

So that's how I happened to be on Holy Isle, to my great surprise, with Lama Yeshi and a television crew and some other hangers-on who were warned sternly to keep out of camera-range and not to talk too loudly. Obeying this instruction, we crept off in the direction of the lighthouse, whispering what a lovely day it was. Even whispers sounded loud. The quiet over there is as deep as a well and Arran by comparison sounds like a noisy beehive, all abuzz with bus engines.

St Molio's cave had graffiti on it. Nothing obscene—just initials, but it was upsetting all the same, specially as there was a very clearly marked 'AP'. Please Miss it wisnae me. I've never been here, Miss, honest. That's one of the troubles about being a Green person—you feel obscurely responsible for the nastiness of the human race. It's bad enough in Glen Ashdale, tutting over the chucked away cans and Marathon wrappers—vandals really do seem to run on peanut power—but on Holy Isle there's a positive sense of desecration.

Lama Yeshi came down the hill in his lemon-yellow wellies and said that something would have to be done to ensure that would-be meditators who came for a people-free retreat were not disturbed. I promptly changed sides and started to worry about all the nature-loving folk on Arran who have felt deprived of a chance to go to Holy Isle all these years, and said so. Lama Yeshi smiled.

Now there is something about Lama Yeshi's smile that is utterly disarming. I had expected to be somewhat in awe of him and that he would have a look-to-the-horizon calm which would seem above all our mundane frettings, but I was completely unprepared for dimples. He smiles with utter infectious happiness and it causes an odd little inward flutter, as if one was very young again and the trunk was being packed to go on holiday.

The next day Holy Isle had retreated into the blowing rain like a grey shadow of its former self but off they all went again, maroon robes and yellow wellies and cagoules and got thoroughly soaked, chugging round the island in a small boat and landing in unorthodox places and scrambling up hills. Did they still like it? 'Oh yes,' they said. 'Even better.' Lama Yeshi had decided that there was room on the island for everyone as long as people respect each other and stay away from areas which are reserved for absolutely uninterrupted tranquillity. It seems reasonable.

Inevitably, the larger newspapers got interested in the story. The *Guardian* carried a facetious piece which made it quite clear that the writer's view of island life was based on a half-forgotten viewing of *Whisky Galore*. The poor soul. There he was, trying hard to be funny in some office in London, while we were being followed along the edge of the sea by a robin that hopped from stone to stone, and the clean water ran chuckling down the hill. There was snow on Arran's peaks and yet the sun shone warmly.

There will be a lot of misunderstanding and a lot of idle curiosity from people who do not understand the bond which can exist between people and the place they live in. To 'fall in love with Arran' means the reason why most people come here and stay here. The Buddhists have fallen in love with Holy Isle and that is the best possible start. Lama Yeshi's smile will do the rest.

Alison Prince (b.1931) *Arran Banner* 30 November 1991. Reprinted in *On Arran* (Argyll Publishing, 1994)

Thinking of Coire Fhionn Lochan
Carl MacDougall, 1996

Later, when we'd remade the bed and drawn the curtains, when we had brushed our teeth and were ready for sleep, I was thinking of Coire Fhionn Lochan, up the hill from North Thundergay on the Isle of Arran, dark and still at the head of a brae, in a horseshoe of hills. It was impossible to tell the reality from reflection, the water like plastic, bearing the strain of light, the glitter of stones and pebbles shining from below the resin; the air still as stone, suddenly clear after four days of cloud.

Carl MacDougall (b.1941) *The Casanova Papers* (Secker & Warburg, 1996)

The Old Song
James McGonigal, 1997

I'm not much haunted by the dead (more by the living,
folk I'll never see, having at one time loved or held them
and let go—or they did, who knows, we'll not speak again)
but maybe there was one time, crossing Machrie Moor,
returning with the children from the standing stones.

Standing Stones on Machrie Moor by F. Noel-Paton (Art Journal, July 1885)

I was thinking (more or less: better say the thought
came to me) that the light was failing and we should
be home. Just over that next heathery rise would be
the sea. Or else this next one. Still no sight or sound:
and then the smell of peat reek. Against an orange sky

black huts half sunk in earth and smoothly turfed.
I knew there'd be a welcome for a traveller returning
after months away, with news, a song, some seeds.
Not yet my home ground, but the people here would
know me: and so I bent to enter the first house

pulling the skin hap back from the doorpost.
All of that's nonsense, naturally. I was tired
and the light was poor. Anxious to make sure
we reached the sea and then the coast road home.
It's just that movement that I can't forget, bending

to pull aside the leather hap from the door
with my left hand. That, and the weight
of the seedbag and the song I still
sometimes nearly start to sing:
'The Lost King'.

James McGonigal (b.1947) 1997

Postscript

THE BEACH, LAMLASH.

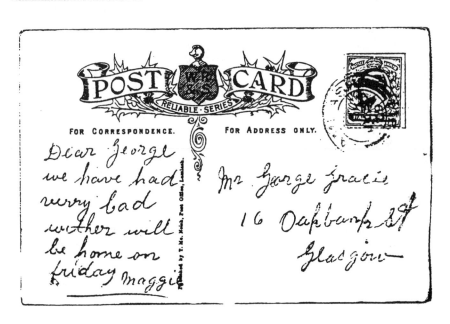

Dear George
we have had
very bad
wither will
be home on
friday Maggie

Mr George Gracie
16 Oakbank St
Glasgow

Glossary

abune, above
Anakim, Biblical race of giants inhabiting
  Mount Hebron

balloch, narrow mountain pass
beild, shelter
bien, well-to-do, comfortable, pleasant
bocans, hobgoblins
brae, upland area, steep bank
buirdly, burly, rough
but, without

cairry, burden; sky
chaulmer, chamber
chinner, grumble
clachan, hamlet
cole, haycock
corbies, crows
cowp, rubbish heap
crack, screech
cruttle, crumb, fragment
cunings, rabbits

darg, work
dawds, lumps
divot, turf
douce, respectable, neat, comfortable
dree their weird, endure their fate
drouth, drought; thirst

eerie, frightened, uneasy

fanks, sheepfolds
flaggs, coarse grass

fluke, flounder
fulyery, foliage

gang, go
gert, caused
gill, gull
girn, whine
gled, buzzard; kite
gloamin', dusk
greit, cry
guidsir, grandfather

haddie, haddock
hairst, harvest
hallie, hollow
holm, low lying land beside a river
houlac, Gael. *chuileag*, gnat
howkit, hollowed out

ilk, each, every

jean, toffee
kelpies, water demons

Kerrigan, name given to orphans
  farmed out to farmers and to non-
  native residents (orig. a land worker
  of Irish stock)—Arran usage
kye, cows

ling, heather; deer grass
linns, waterfalls
lown, sheltered
lowp, leap

maik, halfpenny
mirk, dark
Mona, Isle of Man
muir, moor

Nabal, miserly person (after Nabal in I
    Samuel)
niffer, barter, trade

poddlie, tadpole; minnow
prutchie, call to cows
pyet, oyster catcher
pykit, picked

rairin, roaring
raun, roe
raun, rowan
redd, fish-spawn
rickle, loose heap or pile
rowe, roll
rude, cross
run rig, system of joint holding of strips
    of land

sarkin, roof boarding
saughs, willows
scadans, thin turf, top paring of peat
schlaried, smeared
scuddy, naked
shaw, thicket
shielings, huts
skrech, screech
slaps, openings
smoored, smothered
sperit, asked
sted, steading
steer, bustle
stob, stake, post
sturt, strife, trouble
syne, then

tent, look after
thack, thatch
thackit, thatched
trummle, tremble
tuim, empty
tummelt, tumbled
tups, rams

wame, belly
whaup, curlew
winnock, window

yird, earth
yowe, ewe

Notes

'**Arran of the Many Stags**' (p. 1). There is also a verse translation by Professor Kuno Meyer in J.K. Cameron's *The Church in Arran* and a good prose translation by Kenneth Jackson in his *A Celtic Miscellany* (Penguin, 1971).

John Barbour (pp. 1-4). In 1307 Bruce used Arran as a staging post in his campaign to regain Scotland. The 'narrow place' and 'woody glen' where Douglas's men camped is supposed to have been Glen Cloy. And Bruce, of course, is said to have lodged with a spider in what is now known as King's Cave, Drumadoon.

Martin Martin (pp. 7-11). Author, traveller and a factor in Skye, Martin visited Arran in 1695.

'**Goat milk quarters**' (p. 11). Goat's milk was fashionably drunk for its supposed health-giving properties.

Thomas Pennant (pp. 11-15). Welsh naturalist and indefatigable traveller. He slightly misquotes his Vergil (*Aeneid* I, 159-60)—there is no 'Hic' ('An island forms a harbour by opposition of its sides').

[Mr Hutchison] (pp. 16-18). James Inglis in *Brodick—Old and New* gives the Glasgow merchant's name as Hutchison but without any source.

James Headrick (pp. 18-22). Visited Arran in 1803.

John Phillips (p. 24). Became Professor of Geology at London, Dublin and Oxford and wrote *Life on the Earth: Its Origin and Succession* in 1860. The manuscript journal of his Scottish tour is filled with sketches, both topographical and geological.

John Wilson (p. 29). Timothy Tickler—character based on Wilson's uncle, Robert Sym; Shepherd—the poet, James Hogg. Taken from *Noctes Ambrosianae*, a series of imaginary conversations set in William Ambrose's Edinburgh tavern.

John Paterson (pp. 30-31). The Duke of Hamilton's factor, infamous for organizing the Arran clearances. He won a silver medal for this essay.

Elizabeth King (pp. 31-33). 'Willie' was of course William Thomson (1824-1907), later Lord Kelvin, born in Belfast but brought up in Glasgow following his father's appointment as Professor of Mathematics. Elizabeth was his sister.

Lord Teignmouth (pp. 34-36). As well as visiting Arran he was also Governor-General of India.

Elvira Phipps (pp. 36-37). Her ascent of Goatfell took place in 1840.

Andrew Ramsay (pp. 37-38). Born in Glasgow. Director-General of the Geological Survey.

Brodick Fair (pp. 42-43). Another good description of the fair can be found in John Sillars, *The Brothers* (1924), chapter 5.

Alexander Smith (pp. 50-52). Smith's holiday in Arran took place in July 1848. He was accompanied by a friend, Thomas Brisbane. See Brisbane's memoir, *The Early Years of Alexander Smith* (Hodder & Stoughton, 1869), chapter 4.

John Fergusson (pp. 52-53). The lighthouse on Pladda was built in 1790 and rebuilt in 1825.

Thomas Alexander (pp. 54-55). *Charles Gordon* is a romantic novel set in Glasgow about 1853.

Lewis Carroll (pp. 56-57). Carroll was at this time trying to persuade the artist Sir Joseph Noel Paton (1821-1901) to illustrate *Through the Looking-glass*. He eventually gave up and used John Tenniel.

William Mitchell (pp. 57-63). A merchant who lived at 12 Kew Terrace, Glasgow.

William Lytteil (pp. 63-65). The Picture Cave is about 900 yards to the north-west of the Cock Farm.

John T. Reid (pp. 65-67). In 1991 the author and artist Mairi Hedderwick followed in Reid's footsteps in a then-and-now tour, even attempting a version of his 'design of starting at dead of night for a walk round the north of the island'.

William McQueen (pp. 67-70). A Glasgow journalist. His gothic reference is to A. Radcliffe's *The Mysteries of Udolpho* (1794).

Arran Murder (pp. 82-87). This was the first case covered by the criminologist William Roughead and it made a great impression on him. He had no doubt about Laurie's guilt. Jack House in his *Murder Not Proven?* (1984) reckoned the verdict should have been Not Proven. Laurie's death sentence was commuted to life imprisonment and he died in 1930.

Charles E. Hall (pp. 88-91). The ancient ancestor of the title is the legendary poet Ossian (said to be buried at Clachaig), from whom Malvina Fergusson, the heroine of this 3-decker romantic novel, set largely in the Kilmory area, claims descent. The plot also involves a search for the lost original manuscripts used by James Macpherson in his 'translations' of Ossian. Bernard Drake is a young artist camping on the Lagg shore to be near his love, Malvina, who is staying at Clachaig.

George Milner (pp. 90-94). His book is an account of an August holiday at Corrie.

George Eyre-Todd (pp. 94-97). One of the earliest books by this now almost forgotten Scottish man of letters was a romantic medieval tale in verse, *The Lady of Ranza* (1894).

Stazel Dene (p. 100). *The Gortchen* is an odd Arran kailyard tale (full of local characters) about a foundling boy, a 'Kerrigan', brought up on the croft of Gortchenland.

William Brown (p. 102). This verse has been set to music by James Pattinson.

Paddy Coffey (pp. 103-4). He was known as the Glasgow Harbour Bard.

Neil Munro (pp. 104-07). From his 'Looker-On' column. Arran references can also be found throughout his Para Handy tales.

'R.M. Featherpick' (pp. 107-08). *Arran in Spring* is a record of visits to Arran made annually for over 50 years by men who were fellow students at Glasgow University: Walter W. Blackie, Harry McEwen, Charles Ker, J.W. Birrell, Charles E. Beckett and others. This parody of 'Sir Patrick Spens' is from 1923.

John Sillars (pp. 109-13). Sillars, who was born near Corriegills and lived most of his life in Lamlash, is Arran's only indigenous novelist. *The Desperate Battle* tells the story of three generations of an Arran family. Robert McLellan felt it was 'a genuine record of Arran life, written with humour and compassion... achieving in its central character, based on the author's mother, a triumph of portraiture. The desperate battle of the title is her struggle to rear her family.' (*The Isle of Arran*, chapter 7). 'Park' is Corriegills.

James Nicol (pp. 114-15). His book also contains a verse tribute to the potato pioneer Donald MacKelvie, written on the occasion of a dinner in his honour in the Douglas Hotel on 20 November 1925. Nicol was an Arran stonemason.

J.J. Bell (pp. 115-16). Famous as the creator of the pawky Glasgow urchin, Wee Macgreegor. In *I Remember* (1932) he recalls a holiday spent on Arran.

Margaret Hamilton (pp. 122-25). *Bull's Penny* traces a man's life over 80 years, from childhood in a lightly disguised Arran ('Ramma') to Glasgow in the 1930s. 'Shennadale' is Lamlash.

George Blake (pp. 125-29). Best known for his novel of the Depression, *The Shipbuilders* (1935).

Robert McLellan (pp. 130-35). 'Arran Burn' was commissioned by BBC Television as one of their Television Poems (others were Alexander Scott on Aberdeen, Robert Garioch on Edinburgh, Tom Wright on Glasgow and Norman MacCaig on Assynt), and first broadcast on 2 December 1965, produced by Finlay J. Macdonald. The poem was read by Ian Cuthbertson to accompany still photographs by Alan Daiches. It was broadcast again on 2 December 1966 with film of the island.

Archie Roy (pp. 135-39). *Deadlight* is a Buchanesque thriller set mainly on Arran. Roger Arnott of Glasgow University discovers a 'secret so powerful that it could change the future of mankind.' The Arran landscape is used to great effect.

Robin Fulton (pp. 141-42). Born on Arran; his father was minister at Shiskine. The first of the Arran haiku was published in *Oasis* 28, 1979.

Edwin Morgan (p. 144). 'Arran Potatoes' is based on the varieties grown at the Arran Heritage Museum in the summer of 1985. See also his poem 'Nineteen Kinds of Barley', based on the Barley Variety Demonstration in the field at Bungalow Road, Lamlash, summer of 1984.

Bibliography and Further Reading

Aitken, William. 'The Arran Post' (poem) in his *Rhymes and Readings* (Glasgow, 1880)

'Ajax'. 'Vacation' (poem) in *High School of Glasgow Magazine* June 1937

Alexander, Thomas. *Charles Gordon; or, The Mask of Friendship. A Tale of Real Life* (Glasgow, 1865)

Alexander, Tom. *Remember When We Lived on Arran: Some recollections of life on Arran between the years 1947-1984* (Edinburgh: Tom Alexander, 1986)

Allerton, Mark. 'The Lion Hunters: An Incident at Whiting Bay' (*The People's Friend* 8 August 1904)

Anonymous. *The Isle of Arran: A Poem*. Cantos I and II (Edinburgh: Fraser, 1848)

———. 'The musings in idle hours of an Arran Rustic' (manuscript poem, Cowie Collection, Mitchell Library, Glasgow)

———. 'Sweet Arran's Isle' (Glasgow: Poet's Box, 1859)

Arran Banner 1974- (weekly newspaper published in Brodick)

Arran Children Writing: A selection of the entries to the Arran Children's Creative Writing Competition ([Brodick:] Isle of Arran Film Society, [1967]; printed at the Gallery Press, Whiting Bay) (Winners chosen by Edwin Morgan)

The Arran Naturalist 1978- (Isle of Arran Natural History Society)

The Arran Tragedy. Life and trial of Laurie, with lessons of the crime (Glasgow, 1889)

Arran Women's Rural Institute. *History of the Villages of Arran* [1975] (revised 1983)

Ayr Observer 29 June 1847

Baddeley, M.J.B. & Jordan, E.D. *Black's Guide to the Clyde* (London: A. & C. Black, 1897)

Balfour, J.A., ed. *The Book of Arran [Vol.I]: Archaeology* (Glasgow: Hugh Hopkins for the Arran Society of Glasgow, 1910. Reprinted 1982 by Kilbrannan Publishing, Brodick)

Banks, Iain. *The Bridge* (London: Macmillan, 1986)

Barbour, John. *The Bruce, being the Metrical History of Robert the Bruce King of Scots*, translated by George Eyre-Todd (Glasgow: Gowans & Gray, 1907)

Barton, William. 'A Visit to Glencloy, At Arran' in his *Poems* (Glasgow, 1879)

Beckett, James. *The Tourist's Guide to Arran* (Edinburgh and Glasgow: Menzies, Porteous and Thomas Murray, 1888)

155

Bell, John Joy. *I Remember* (Edinburgh: Porpoise Press, 1932)

———. *Scotland's Rainbow West* (London: Harrap, 1933)

Black, C. Stewart. *The Guinea's Stamp: a gentle satire on Glasgow society* (Glasgow: Brown Son & Ferguson, [1927]) (Scottish Plays No.2) (Set in Whiting Bay)

Blackie, John Stuart. 'Glen Rosa' and 'A sabbath meditation' (poems) in his *Lays of the Highlands and Islands* (London: Walter Scott, 1888)

Blake, George. *The Firth of Clyde* (London: Collins, 1952)

Boyle, Andrew. *Pictorial History of Arran* (Darvel: Alloway Publishing, 1994)

Brotchie, T.C.F. *Scottish Western Holiday Haunts* (Glasgow and Edinburgh: John Menzies, 1911)

Brown, William. *Gleniffer and Glen Rosa and other poems* (Paisley: Alexander Gardner, 1912)

Bruce, George. 'Boarding House, Arran' and 'Coach Tour and Locals' in his *Collected Poems* (Edinburgh: Edinburgh University Press, 1971)

Bryce, James. *The Geology of Arran and the other Clyde Islands* 4th ed. (Glasgow and London: Collins, 1872)

'BUC'. 'Row saftly, proud ocean' (poem) in James Lemon, ed., *Lays of St Mungo*, 2nd series (Glasgow: Smith & Watson, 1845)

Buchanan, George. *The History of Scotland*, translated by James Aikman (Glasgow and Edinburgh, 1827)

Buchanan, George. *Tour Round Arran* (Glasgow, [1883])

Burgess, Moira. 'The Adjacent Islands: Literary Associations of the County of Bute' (*Library Review* 19:7, Autumn 1964)

Burrel, John. *Journals, 1766-1782* (Brodick, 1982)

Cameron, Rev. J. Kennedy. *The Church in Arran* (Edinburgh: John Grant, 1912)

Campbell, Donald. 'A Sense of Community: Robert McLellan: An Appreciation' (*Chapman* 43-44, Spring 1986)

Campbell, Franthony [Frances and Anthony]. *Milestones of Arran* (Brodick: Isle of Arran Tourist Organisation, [1979])

Campbell, George. Verse Letter on Pirnmill, 1909 (printed in the *Arran Banner* 8 February 1997)

Campsie, Alistair. 'Trials and tribulations of an aspiring author' (*Glasgow Herald* 25 May 1985)

Carmichael, Alexander. *Carmina Gadelica*, vol. II (Edinburgh and London: Oliver and Boyd, 1928)

Carroll, Lewis. *The Diaries of Lewis Carroll*, edited by L.R. Green (London: Cassell, 1954)

Claridge, Marten. *Slow Burn* (London:Headline, 1994)

Clark, Thomas A. *Coire Fhionn Lochan* (Nailsworth: Moschatel Press, 1990)

Cockburn, Henry, Lord. *Circuit Journeys* (Edinburgh: David Douglas, 1888)

Coffey, Paddy. *Pickings from the Poetical Works* (Edinburgh & Glasgow: John Menzies, [1920])

Cook, George H. ed. *Memorial to the Arran Clearances* (Saint John, New Brunswick, 1977)

Cowley, Colin. *Arran Books File* (Lamlash, 1990)

———. *Arran Historical Quiz* (Lamlash, 1989)

———. *Arran Ships File* (Lamlash, 1989)

———. *Supernatural Arran* (Lamlash, 1989)

Crocket, K.V. and Walker, A. *Arran, Arrochar & The Southern Highlands* ([Edinburgh:] Scottish Mountaineering Trust, 1989)

Currie, Ronald. *The Place-Names of Arran* (Glasgow: John Smith, 1908)

Davidson, Rev. P. (of Brodick). *Poems on Various Religious Subjects* (Glasgow, 1877) (In Gaelic and English)

Dene, Stazel. *The Gortchen: A Tale of an Arran Glen* (London: Bigby, Long & Co., 1898)

Donoghue, Daniel. 'When I had Laurie of Arran fame for Chum' (*Weekly Record* 8 August 1925)

Downie, R. Angus. *All About Arran* (London and Glasgow: Blackie, 1933)

Eyre-Todd, George. *The Island of Arran*, with drawings by Robert Eadie (Glasgow: Walter Wilson, 1921)

———. *The Lady of Ranza* (Paisley & London: Alexander Gardner, 1884)

———. 'The splendid island' in his *Leaves from the Life of a Scottish Man of Letters* (Glasgow: Brown Son and Ferguson, 1934)

———. *Vignettes of the North* (Glasgow: Morison Brothers, 1895)

Fairhurst, Horace. *Exploring Arran's Past* (Glasgow: Central Press, 1981. Revised ed., Kilbrannan Publishing, Brodick, 1982)

Ferguson, James. *Four Views in the Isle of Arran* (Edinburgh, 1842)

Fergusson, John. *Poems: consisting of a series of interesting subjects; scenes and traditions in Arran; elegies, and other detached pieces* (Ayr, Irvine and Glasgow, 1849)

Fernie, Mary. *Around the Island of Arran* (Albyn Press, 1985)

———. *Flora in Poetry: Isle of Arran* (Dumfries, 1979)

Fforde, The Lady Jean. *Castles in the Air* (Brodick: Kilbrannan Publishing, 1982. Revised ed., Stuart Titles, Glasgow, 1996)

Firsoff, V.A. *Arran with Camera and Sketchbook* (London: Hale, 1951)

Fulton, Robin. *Selected Poems* (Edinburgh: Macdonald, 1980)

Gardner, Arthur. *Sun, Cloud and Snow in the Western Highlands, from Glencoe to Ardnamurchan, Mull and Arran* (Edinburgh: Grant & Murray, 1933)

Gemmell, Alastair. *Discovering Arran* (Edinburgh: John Donald, 1990)

Gill, Cicely and Prince, Alison. *A Book of Arran Poetry* ([Brodick:] Arran Theatre and Arts Trust Ltd, 1993)

Glasgow Journal 12 March 1759

'Glasgow Pedestrian'. *Our Western Hills, and how to reach them, and the views from their summits* (Glasgow, 1892)

Gow, Robert. 'Arran, 1945' (poem) (*Voice of Scotland* II: 2, December 1945)

Grierson, Thomas. *Autumnal Rambles Among the Scottish Mountains* (Edinburgh, 1850)

Hall, Rev. Charles. *The Isle of Arran* (London: A. & C. Black, 1912. Reprinted 1926) (Beautiful Britain series)

Hall, Charles E. *An Ancient Ancestor: A Tale of Three Weeks* (London: Skeffington, 1893) 3 vols

Hall, Ken. *North Arran—A Postcard Tour* (Ochiltree: Richard Stenlake, 1993)

———. *South Arran—A Postcard Tour* (Ochiltree: Richard Stenlake, 1994)

Hall, Tom S. *Tramping Holidays in Scotland* (London: Country Life, 1933)

———. *Tramping in Arran: A Fellowship Holiday* (Glasgow: James Hedderwick, [1935]. Revised ed., 1947. 4th ed., 1960)

Hamilton, Rev. John. 'Parish of Kilmory' in *Statistical Account of Scotland*, ed. Sir John Sinclair, Vol. 9 (Edinburgh: Creech, 1793)

Hamilton, Margaret. *Bull's Penny* (London: MacGibbon & Kee, 1950)

Hari-Kari [Robert Browning]. *Songs of Two Cities* (Glasgow & Dalbeattie, 1910)

Headrick, Rev. James. *View of the Mineralogy, Agriculture, Manufactures and Fisheries of the Island of Arran...* (Edinburgh: Constable, 1807)

Hedderwick, Mairi. *An Eye on the Hebrides: An Illustrated Journey* (Edinburgh: Canongate, 1989)

———. *Highland Journey: A Sketching Tour of Scotland retracing the footsteps of Victorian artist John T. Reid* (Edinburgh: Canongate, 1992)

Henderson, Angus. 'Highland Notes: A Popular Resort' (*Scots Observer* 3 June 1933)

Hendry, Alasdair. *My Walks of Arran* [Brodick, 1988]

Holmer, Nils M. *The Gaelic of Arran* (Dublin: Dublin Institute for Advanced Studies, 1957)

House, Jack. *Down the Clyde* (Edinburgh & London: Chambers, 1959)

———. 'The Goatfell Case' in his *Murder Not Proven?* (Glasgow: Richard Drew, 1984. Reprinted by Penguin Books, 1989)

Hughes, Thomas. *Memoir of Daniel Macmillan* (London: Macmillan, 1883)

Hutcheson, William. 'Sunset over Goatfell, Arran' (poem) in his *Chota Chants* (Glasgow: Fraser, Edward & Co., 1937)

[Hutchison, —]. 'Journal of a trip to Arran one hundred years ago. Written by a Glasgow merchant' (*Glasgow Evening Times* 1 January 1885. Reprinted in an edition of 25, Kilmarnock, 1901)

Hutchison, Harry. 'The Isle of Arran' (*Scottish Field* August 1963)

Imrie, John. 'The Bonnie Arran Hills' (poem) in his *Songs and Miscellaneous Poems* (Toronto, 1906)

Inglis, James C. *Brodick—Old and New* (Ardrossan: Arthur Guthrie, [1932])

Jeffrey, William. 'Glen Rosa' in his *Selected Poems*, edited by Alexander Scott (Edinburgh: Serif Books, 1951)

Johnston, Donald. *Arran Shipwrecks* (Lamlash: Johnston's Marine Stores, 1994)

Ker, Charles, ed. *Arran in Spring (1879-1937)* (London and Glasgow: Blackie, 1937)

Kerr, Angus G. 'A Place of Summer Pilgrimage: Arran's "Twelve Apostles"' (*Scots Observer* 24 November 1932)

Kerr, James and Ina. 'The Sound of Kilbrannan: An Arran Fantasia and Calendar' (poem) in *Glenburn New Writers* (1978)

King, Elizabeth. *Lord Kelvin's Early Home* (London: Macmillan, 1909)

Knox, Bill. 'Arran aims to be "open" all year' (*The Herald* 8 August 1994)

Kobler, Chris. *Consistent Paradox: 16 poems* (Whiting Bay: Gallery Press [197-])

Landsborough, Rev. David. *Arran: A Poem in Six Cantos* (Edinburgh: Blackwood/ London: Cadell, 1828)

———. *Excursions to Arran, Ailsa Craig and the Two Cumbraes* (Edinburgh: Johnstone and Hunter, 1851)

———. *The Isle of Arran and How to See it* (Ardrossan: Arthur Guthrie/Edinburgh and Glasgow: John Menzies, 1871. Much reprinted)

——— and Landsborough, Rev. David, jun. *Arran: Its Topography, Natural History and Antiquities* (Ardrossan: Arthur Guthrie/London: Houlston, 1875)

Lever, Charles. *Lutrell of Arran* (London: Chapman & Hall, 1854-55)

Lindsay, Alison. 'Penny Foolish & Arran' (*Folly* 16, November 1995)

Lithgow, William. *Travels and Voyages* (Edinburgh, 1770)

Lytteil, William. *Landmarks of Scottish Life and Language* (Edinburgh: J. Moodie Miller, 1877)

McArthur, John. *The Antiquities of Arran...* (Glasgow: Black, 1861. 2nd ed. 1873)

Macbride, Mackenzie. *Arran of the Bens, the Glens & the Brave*, with illustrations in colour by J. Lawton Wingate (London & Edinburgh: T. N. Foulis, 1910)

McBride, Peter Carswell. 'Fair Arran Hills' (poem) in his *Gems of a Wandering Minstrel* (Rutherglen, 1931)

McCrorie, Ian. *The Sea Routes to Arran* (Gourock: Caledonian MacBrayne, 1993)

Macdonald, Hugh. 'Brodick and Lamlash' in his *Days at the Coast* (Glasgow: Robert Lindsay, 1857) (Includes poem 'The Signal of the Bruce', reprinted in *Poetical Works*, 1865)

MacDougall, Carl. *The Casanova Papers* (London: Secker & Warburg, 1996)

Macdowall, Mrs H. S. *An Arran Airing* (Glasgow, 1905)

Macgregor, Alasdair Alpin. *Somewhere in Scotland* (London: Hale, 1948)

Macgregor, Murray. *Excursion Guide to the Geology of Arran* (Glasgow: Geological Society of Glasgow, 1965. 2nd ed., 1972)

Mackenzie, W.M. *The Book of Arran Volume the Second: History and Folklore* (Glasgow: Hugh Hopkins for the Arran Society of Glasgow, 1914. Reprinted 1982 by Kilbrannan Publishing, Brodick)

MacKillop, D.M. *Annals of Megantic County, Quebec* (Lynn, Mass., 1902)

Mac Lachlan, Alexander. *Songs of Arran* (Edinburgh, 1889)

McLellan, Robert. *Ancient Monuments of Arran: Official Guide* (Edinburgh: HMSO, 1977. 2nd ed., revised, 1989)

————. The Isle of Arran (Newton Abbot: David & Charles, 1970. 2nd ed., revised, 1976. 3rd ed., 1985. 4th ed., revised by Norman Newton, 1995) (The Island series)

————. *Sweet Largie Bay and Arran Burn: Two Poems in Scots* (Preston: Akros Publications, 1977) (Shortened version of 'Sweet Largie Bay' printed in *Scottish Field* November 1958)

Macmillan, Rev. Angus. 'Island of Arran: Parish of Kilmorie' in *The New Statistical Account of Scotland*, Vol. v (Edinburgh and London: Blackwood, 1845)

McNaughton, Rev. Allan. 'Island of Arran: Parish of Kilbride' in *The New Statistical Account of Scotland*, Vol. v (Edinburgh and London: Blackwood, 1845)

McQueen, William. 'To parties in search of a cheap holiday' [c.1880] (In cuttings book, *Articles Various*, the Glasgow Collection, Mitchell Library, Glasgow)

Martin, A.S. 'Winter Fishing Off Arran' (poem) in *Scottish Poetry* 5 (Edinburgh University Press, 1970)

Martin, Martin. *A Description of the Western Isles of Scotland* (London: Andrew Bell, 1703)

Meek, Ronald. *Hill Walking in Arran* (Edinburgh: Chambers, 1963. 2nd ed., 1972)

Milne, Allan Paterson. *Arran: An Island's Story* (Brodick: Kilbrannan Publishing, 1982)

Milner, George. *Country Pleasures* (London: Longmans, Green, 1881)

————. *Studies of Nature on the Coast of Arran*, with illustrations by W. Noel Johnson (London: Longmans, Green, 1894)

Mitchell, Gladys. *The Whispering Knights* (London: Michael Joseph, 1980)

Mitchell, William. *A Fortnight on Arran* (Glasgow: Bell and Bain, 1874)

Mitchell-Luker, Berni. *Mitchell-Luker's Arran Bus Book* (Brodick: Kilbrannan Publishing, 1983)

Mitchison, Naomi. *The Alban Goes Out* (Raven Press, 1939. Reprinted in *The Cleansing of the Knife*, Canongate, Edinburgh, 1978)

Molony, E. *Portraits of Islands* (London, 1951)

Monro, Donald. *Description of the Western Isles of Scotland called Hybrides* [1549] (Edinburgh: William Auld, 1774)

Morgan, Edwin. 'An Arran Death' in his *Collected Poems* (Manchester: Carcanet Press, 1990)

———. 'Arran Potatoes' (*Glasgow Magazine 7*, Winter 1985/86)

Morton, H.V. *In Scotland Again* (London: Methuen, 1933)

Moultrie, John. *Poems*. New ed. (London: Macmillan, 1876) 2 vols

Munro, Neil. 'Isle of Arran: Grandeur on Glasgow's Door-Step' (*Glasgow Evening News* 24 September 1923)

Murdoch, Alexander G. *Scotch Readings*, 2nd series (Glasgow: Thomas Morison, 1888)

Newton, Norman, *The Isle of Arran* (Newton Abbot: Pevensey Press, 1995) (Revision of book by Robert McLellan)

Nicol, James. *A Book of Arran Verse* (Ardrossan: Arthur Guthrie, 1930)

O'Grady, Standish, ed. *Silva Gadelica: a Collection of Tales in Irish* (London: Williams and Norgate, 1892)

O'Sullivan, Don. *Arran Midges* (Isle of Arran: Penlea Press, [1975]) (Poems illustrated by Don McNeish)

Paterson, Jeannie Graham. 'Arran' (poem) in her *Short Threads from a Milliner's Needle* (Glasgow: Carter & Pratt, 1894)

Paterson, John. 'Account of the Island of Arran' in *Prize Essays and Transactions of the Highland and Agricultural Society of Scotland*, Vol. xi (Edinburgh and London: Blackwood and Cadell, 1837)

Pennant, Thomas. *A Tour in Scotland and Voyage to the Hebrides* (Chester, 1774)

Phillips, John. *Tour Round Scotland* [1826] (Unpublished manuscript in the Mitchell Library, Glasgow)

Phipps, Elvira Anna. *Memorials of Clutha: or, Pencillings on the Clyde* (London: C. Armand, for the author, 1841)

Pins and Needles: The best of Pins and Needles as published in the Arran Banner *May '82—May '83* (Brodick: Arran Banner, 1983)

Pollock's Dictionary of the Clyde (Glasgow: John Menzies/London: Simpkin, Marshall, 1888)

Poucher, W.A. *Highland Holiday: Arran to Ben Cruachan* (London: Chapman & Hall, 1945)

Prince, Alison. *A Haunting Refrain* (London: Methuen, 1988. Mandarin Teens paperback, 1989) (Short stories)

———. *Having Been in the City: Poems* (Edinburgh: Taranis Books, 1994)

———. *On Arran* (Glendaruel: Argyll Publishing, 1994) (Reprinting of articles from the *Arran Banner*)

————. 'Winter Journal: If this is life, I'm grateful' (*The Scottish Review* 2, April 1995)

Ramsay, Andrew Crombie. *The Geology of the Island of Arran from Original Survey* (Glasgow: Richard Griffin, 1841)

Reid, Alastair. *Weathering* (Edinburgh: Canongate, 1978)

Reid, John T. *Art Rambles in the Highlands and Islands of Scotland* (London and New York: Routledge, 1878)

Rhead, John and Snow, Philip. *Birds of Arran* (Bridgend, Islay: Saker Press, 1994)

Ritchie, Diana. *Tales of Magic, Mystery and the Macabre*, Vol. 1 (Blackwaterfoot: Arran ITACET Service, 1995)

Robertson, John. *Animal Life on the Shores of the Clyde and Forth* (Glasgow, [1890])

Ross, Lynn. 'Co-operative Craft on Arran: Spinning, weaving and knitting' in *Women and Craft* (London: Virago Press, 1987)

————. *Knitting with Handspun* (Whiting Bay: Ross Gill, 1984. Revised ed., 1989) (Traditional patterns from the Isle of Arran)

Roughead, William. 'The Arran Murder' in his *Twelve Scots Trials* (London: William Green, 1913. Reprinted 1995 by Mercat Press, Edinburgh)

————. ed. *Trial of John Watson Laurie (The Arran Murder)* (Edinburgh and London: William Hodge, 1932) (Notable British Trials series)

Roy, Archie. *Deadlight* (London: John Long, 1968. Reprinted by Kilbrannan Publishing, Brodick, 1983 and Apogee Books, Glasgow, 1986)

S., K. 'Sunset Over Goatfell, Arran' (poem) (*Milden Miscellany* 1:3, Summer-Autumn 1948)

St Marketto, C. [C.T. Borrie]. *Trial Trip of the S.S. 'St. George'* (London: Blackie, 1882)

Scotsman 11 November 1889

Scott, A. Boyd. *The East of Arran: A Guide Book for the Young of All Ages* (Paisley: Alexander Gardner, 1919)

Scott, Sir Walter. *The Lord of the Isles* (Edinburgh: Constable, 1815)

Sharp, William. 'The Isle of Arran' (*Art Journal* July 1885)

Shaw, Jane [Jean Evans]. *Penny Foolish* (London: Nelson, 1953) (Children's novel)

Shore, John, Lord Teignmouth. *Sketches of the Coasts and Islands of Scotland...* (London: John Parker, 1836)

Sillars, John. *The Brothers* (Edinburgh: Blackwood, 1924)

————. *The Desperate Battle* (Edinburgh: Blackwood, 1925)

————. *The McBrides: A Romance of Arran* (Edinburgh: Blackwood, 1922. Popular ed., 1924)

Smith, Alexander. *City Poems* (Cambridge: Macmillan, 1857)

Smith, G. S. 'Easter in Arran' (poem) (*Glasgow University Magazine* 76:4, Candlemas 1965)

Smith, J., ed. *Domestic Scenes...in Different Shires of Scotland* (Glasgow: George Gallie, 1947)

Smith, S. Heckstall. *Isle, Ben and Loch from the Clyde to Skye* (London: Edward Arnold, 1932)

Smith, William Brown. *The World Without and Within* (Saltcoats: Archibald Wallace, 1887)

Somerville, A. C. and Stevenson, W., eds. *The Third Statistical Account of Scotland: The County of Bute* (Glasgow: Collins, 1962)

Somerville, Gertrude A. *Love Is Like An Island* (London: Hale, 1987) (Rainbow Romance)

Steven, Campbell. *The Island Hills* (London, 1955)

Stewart, John A. *Loch Ranza, Arran* (Edinburgh: The Author and the Stewart Society, 1949)

Storrie, Margaret C. 'Landholdings and Population in Arran from the Late Eighteenth Century' (*Journal of the School of Scottish Studies* vol. 11, 1967)

Stuart, Rev. Gershom. 'Parish of Kilbride in Arran' in *The Statistical Account of Scotland*, edited by Sir John Sinclair, vol. 8 (Edinburgh: Creech, 1793)

Swindale, Owen. *Arran Sketches for Two Oboes and Cor Anglais or Bassoon* (Leicester: Phylloscopus Publications, 1993)

Thomson, William. *Leddy May and other poems*, 2nd ed. (Glasgow, 1883)

Waddell, P. Hately. *Ossian and the Clyde: Fingal in Ireland, Oscar in Iceland or Ossian Historical and Authentic* (Glasgow: Maclehose, 1875)

Wallace, W.M.M. *Arran* (Edinburgh: Scottish Mountaineering Trust, 1958. New series, 1970. Revised with supplement, 1979) (Climbers' Guide Books)

Walton, R.D. *Arran in Pictures* (The Author, n.d.)

———. *Seventy Walks in Arran* (Dumfries, 1976. 5th printing, revised, 1985)

Watt, William. 'The Maid of Arran' (song) in his *Poems on Sacred and Other Subjects; and Songs, Humorous and Sentimental* 3rd ed. (Glasgow: The widow of the author, 1860)

Welsh, Mary. *Forty-four Walks on the Isle of Arran* (Kendal: Westmoreland Gazette, 1989)

Whyte, Hamish. *Siva in Lamlash* (Edinburgh: minimal missives, 1991) (poems)

Wilson, John. 'Noctes Ambrosianae' No. XLVI (*Blackwood's Magazine* September 1829)

Wilson, John T. *Heron on the Shore* (Goudhurst, Kent: Weavers Press, 1982) (poems)

Wingate, David. 'Lochranza. An Ejaculative Poem' in his *Poems and Songs* (Glasgow: Kerr & Richardson, 1883)

Wordsworth, William. 'On the Frith of Clyde' in *The Poems*, ed. Thomas Hutchinson (Oxford University Press, 1911)

Index

A'Chir, 138, 139
Adams, Dr, 85, 86-87
Aikman, James, 6
Aitchison, Craigie, xv
Alban Goes Out, The, 116
Alexander, Thomas, 54
Animals, 13, 14, 20-21
Ardrossan, 38, 101, 102, 115
Arran: a Poem (1828), 25
Arran Banner, xiii
'Arran Burn', 130
'Arran Haiku', 142
Arran Murder, The, 82
'Arran of the Many Stags', 1
'Arran Potatoes', 144
'Arran Smacks, The', 103
Auchagallon, 73
Auchencar, 70, 73
Ayr Observer, 42

Ballarie, 118
Ballymeanoch, 8
Banks, Iain, 144
Barbour, John, 1
Barclay, Baron of Ardrossan, 101-2
Barytes, 41
Basking shark, 12
Beinn a'Chliabhain, 139
Beinn Bharrain, 28, 137, 142
Beinn Bhreac, 142
Beinn Nuis, 34, 58, 59, 136-7, 139, 142
Beinn Tarsuinn, 58, 137, 138-9, 142
Bell, J.J., 115
Ben Ghoil *see* Goatfell
Benlister Glen, 126

Bennan, 97-99
Bennan, East, 97
Bennan, West, 97
Bennan Head, 72
Birds, 13, 24, 52
Blackwaterfoot, 54, 73, 127-8, 142
Blake, George, 125
Bleeding, 13, 19
Blue Bell, 94
Boat-house, 65-66
Borrie, C.T., 76
Boyd, Sir Robert, 2
Brambles, 118-20
Brodick, 7, 17, 24, 26, 32, 39-42, 43-44, 65, 75, 78-81, 82, 100, 105, 107, 125-6
Brodick Castle, 2, 6, 7, 9, 39, 75
Brodick Castle, 75
Brodick Fair, 42-43
Brotchie, T.C.F., 101
Brown, William, 102
Browning, Robert, xiv
Browning, Robert ('Hari-Kari'), 101
Bruce, George, 140
Bruce, Robert, King, 1-4, 23, 28
Buchanan, George, 6
Buddhists, 146-7
Bungalow Road, Lamlash, 143
Burns, Robert, xiv-xv

Caeilte, 1
Caisteall Abhail, 12, 13
Campbell, John, 91-92
Campbeltown, 119
Carlyle, Thomas, xiv
Carmichael, Alexander, 97

Carradale, 116, 117
Carroll, Lewis, 56
Catacol, 69, 73
Cattle, 9, 14, 21, 49, 76-78, 133
Ceum na Caillich, 27
Chaleur Bay, New Brunswick, 107
Chalmadale, 137
Churches, 10, 32
Cioch na h-Oighe, 26-27, 28, 106
Cir Mhor, 27, 28, 58, 59, 60, 108
Clark, Thomas A., 145
Clearances, 35, 36, 107, 132
Climate, 13, 22
'Coach Tour and Locals', 140
Cock of Arran, 65, 106, 121
Cockburn, Henry, Lord, 38
Coffey, Paddy, 103
Coire Fhionn Lochan, 37-38, 145, 147
'Common Things like Stick Gathering,
    Tinker Folk and House-Cleaning', 109
Cook family, 53, 72, 99-100
Cordon, 71
Corrie, 13, 62, 74, 78, 83, 91-92, 93-94,
    105, 106, 107, 108, 142
Corriegills, 24, 70, 109-13
Crawford, Sandy, 36-37
Crops, 14, 22, 49
Cuithe, 65

Davaar island, 137
Deer, 1, 9, 13, 130
Dene, Stazel, 100
Dippin Lodge, 71
Distilling, 31, 34
Dougarie Lodge, 73, 104
Douglas, Sir James, 1-4
Druim-a-ghinnir, 99
Drumadoon, 4, 7, 73
Dunbar, L.M., 86-87
Dunfion, 24, 70
Dunn, Alastair, xv

Eagles, 13
Eardley, Joan, xv
Eas Bàn, 78
Eyre-Todd, George, 94

Fairies, 99-100
Fairs, 42-43, 66-67
Fallen Rocks, 107

Farming, 35, 48-49
'Featherpick, R.M.', 107
Feorline, 73
Fergusson, John, 52
Fionn, 7, 8
Fishing, 45-47, 56, 68, 116-7, 140
'Flying Over Arran', 141
Fullarton family, 9-10, 33
Fulton, Robin, 141-2
Furze, Carol, xv

Gaelic, xv, 10, 20, 44, 96
Garbh Allt, 58, 136
Geology, 24, 85
Girl Jean, 140
Glaister, 135
Glasgow Herald, 85
Glasgow Journal, 11
Glen Ashdale, 146
Glen Chalmadale, 74, 92-93, 106-7
Clen Cloy, 43, 106
Glen Iorsa, 60, 106, 137, 138
Glen Rosa, 26, 28, 39, 41, 43, 57-59, 106
Glen Sannox, 27-28, 41, 50-52, 57, 60-62,
    74, 82, 86, 106, 108
Glen Shurig, 48, 106
Glenalbin, 31, 33
Glenkill House, 56
Goatfell, 6, 11, 13, 23, 24, 28, 34, 36-37,
    39, 40-41, 43, 49-50, 61, 74, 76, 82-87,
    100, 107, 142,
'Goatfell', 63
Goats, 13, 14
Goats' milk, 11, 13
Gruagach, The, 97-99

Hall, Charles E., 88
Hamilton, Anne, Duchess of, 7, 15, 19,
    21
Hamilton, James, 2nd Marquis of, 6
Hamilton, Lindsay, xv
Hamilton, Margaret, 122
Hamilton, Dukes of, 9, 13, 18, 30, 33, 35,
    39, 104, 105, 115
'Hamish at the Glen', 100
Harvest, 88-89, 112
Hastings, Sir John, 2
Headrick, Rev. James, xv, 18
Hedderwick, Mairi, xv
Hillside Cottage, 73

Hogg, James, 29
Hollow of the Dead, 118-20
Holy Isle, 4, 6, 20, 26, 66, 71, 126, 127, 146-7
Horses, 13, 14, 20-21
Hutchison, Mr, 16

Imachar, 70, 73
Invercloy, 31
Iorsa Water, 47, 137
Ireland, 1
'Isle of Arran', 140
Isle of Arran: A Poem (1848), 48
'Isle of Arran: Grandeur on Glasgow's Doorstep', 104

John of Islay, 4

Keats, John, xiv
Kent, 53
Ker, W.P., xiv
Kilbrannan Sound, 68, 73, 106, 116-7
Kilbride, 4
Kildonan, 16, 101-2, 105, 106
Kildonan Castle, 4
Kilmichael, 7, 8
Kilmory, 4, 88-91
Kilpatrick Point, 73
King, Elizabeth, 31
King's Cave, 54, 73
Kintyre, 2, 3, 73, 137
'Kirn-Supper, The', 88
'Kye Song, The', 76

Lagg, 16, 54
Lagg Hotel, 88, 89-91
Lamlash, 6, 8, 15, 17, 20, 24, 26, 32, 42, 56-57, 66, 71, 92, 101, 103, 105, 107, 122-5, 126, 143
Lamlash churchyard, 76
Lamlash Fair, 66-67, 122-3
Landsborough, Rev. David, xv, 25
Landsborough, Rev. David, jun., xv
Laurie, John Watson, 82-87
Lindsay, Rev. Mr, 13
Lithgow, William, 7, 107
Lochranza, 9, 11-12, 23, 69, 73-74, 85, 118-20, 122, 128
Lochranza Castle, 4, 12, 73-74
'Lodgings at Arran', 78

Logan, Francis, 83
Lord of the Isles, The, 23
Lytteil, William, 63

MacAlastair, Donald, 99
McBride, Janet, 93
McCulloch, Horatio, xv
Macdonalds of the Isles, 10
MacDougall, Carl, 147
McGlosher, Sandy, 92
McGonigal, James, 147
MacGregor, Alasdair Alpin, 118
Machrie, 8, 106, 135
Machrie Moor, 147
Machrie Water, 7, 8, 14, 45, 46-47, 73, 136
Mackinnon, Mr, 35-36
Mac Lachlan, Alexander, 76
McLellan, Robert, xiv, xv, 130
McNeil, Martha, 65-66
McNiven, Willie, 94
McPhail, Shon, 103-4
McQueen, William, 67
Mann, Lesley, xv
Maol Donn, 78
Martin, Martin, 7
Meikle Stane, 78
Meikleham, Professor William, 32
Merkland Point, 75
Midges, 47
Millar, Margaret, 10
Milner, George, 91
Mitchell, William, 57
Mitchison, Naomi, 116
Monamore Burn, 102
Monamore Glen, 126
Monastery, 4
Monro, Dean Donald, 4
Monyquil, 17, 135
More, John, 93
Morgan, Edwin, 144
Munro, Neil, 104
Murdoch, Alexander G., 78

Nicol, James, 114
North Glen Sannox, 92, 120-1
North Thundergay, 147
Nuts, 1, 120-1

O'Grady, Standish H., 1
'Old Song, The', 147

'On the Frith of Clyde', 29
Ossian, 72

'Park' (Corriegills), 109-13
Paterson, John, xv, 30
Paton, Sir Noel, xv, 56
Pennant, Thomas, 11, 19
Penrioch, 73
Phillips, John, 24
Phipps, Elvira Anna, 36
Picture Cave, 63-65
Pier dues, 114
Pirnmill, 67-70, 73, 117
Pladda, 4, 6, 52-53, 72
Population, 18
Potatoes, 111, 112, 144
Prince, Alison, xv, 146
Puffers, 122
Purdie, Hugh, xv

'Ramble Round Arran, A', 70
Ramsay, Andrew Crombie, 37
Religion, 10, 18, 30, 32, 35-36, 43-44, 92,
    93, 131, 133
Reid, Alistair, 140
Reid, John T., xv, 65
Rhuba Airigh Bheirg, 73
Roads, 21-22
Roman, 122
Rose, Edwin, 82-86
Ross, The, 102
Roughead, William, 87
Roy, Archie, 135

Saddle, The, 100, 108
St Molaise, 20, 146
St Patrick, 1
Salmon, 132-3
Sanda, 137
Sannox, 13, 27
Sannox Water, 107
Saturday Review, 105
Scotsman, 82
Scott, A. Boyd, 105
Scott, Sir Walter, 23
'Servant of the Lord', 122
Sheep, 9, 14, 21, 49, 50, 94-97, 131, 132
'Sheep-Shearing in Arran', 94
'Shennadale' (Lamlash), 122-5
Shiskine, 16-17, 48-49, 107, 142

Shore, John, Lord Teignmouth, 34
Shore House, 16
Sillars, John, 109
'Siva in Lamlash', 143
Sleeping Warrior, 125, 144
Sliddery, 72, 106
Smallpox, 19
Smith, Alexander, 50
Smith, J., 43
Smith, William Brown, 70
Snakes, 21
Spinning, 93
Springbank, 17
Standing stones, 8, 15, 73, 147
Strathwhillan, 75
Steamers, 25, 29, 31, 33, 67-68, 72, 75, 144
Stoddart, Dr, 19
String Road, 17, 135
Suidhe Fhearghas, 27, 86
Superstitions, 19, 31
'Sweet Arran's Isle', 55

Tea, 36
Thomson, James, 85-86
Thomson, William, 63
Thomson, William (Lord Kelvin), 32
Thundergay, 34, 73
Thundergay, North, 147
Tinkers, 110-1
'To an Arran Piermaster', 114
Tobacco, 36
Tormore, 14, 73

Urie Loch, 102

'Victim Running', 135

Walker, Mrs, 82, 83, 84-85
Weaving, 69
Whitefarland Point, 73
Whiting Bay, 16, 71, 126-7, 142
Whyte, Hamish, 143
'Wild Monamore', 102
Wilson, John, 29
Witches' Bridge, 92-93
Wordsworth, William, 29

Yeshi, Lama, 146-7